The SPIRITUAL LEGACY of
John F. Kennedy

JANICE T. CONNELL

Other Books by Janice T. Connell

The Spiritual Journey of George Washington

Faith of Our Founding Father

Queen of the Cosmos

The Visions of the Children

Triumph of the Immaculate Heart

Angel Power

Prayer Power

Miracles of Prayer

Meetings with Mary

The Secrets of Mary

Praying with Mary

Queen of Angels

Christ Through Mary

Mary Seat of Wisdom

The SPIRITUAL LEGACY of John F. Kennedy
Copyright © 2025 by Janice T. Connell

Published by Four Winds Publishing LLC

Cover and Interior Design: GKS Creative
Copyediting and Proofreading: Monti Shalosky
Project Management: The Cadence Group

Hardcover ISBN: 978-1-7372170-6-0

Paperback ISBN: 978-1-7372170-7-7

eISBN: 978-1-7372170-8-4

All rights reserved. No portion of this book may be reproduced, stored in an electronic retrieval system, or transmitted in any form or by any means – electronic, mechanical, photocopy, recording, or any other – except for brief quotations in printed reviews, without the prior written permission of the publisher.

The author hereby affirms unconditional submission to the Magisterium

This book is dedicated to John F. Kennedy and all brave patriots living, deceased, and yet to be born who in any way lend their hearts, skills, strength, and prayers to protect and defend the ideals of the United States of America. May their courage maintain peaceful life, liberty and the pursuit of happiness so that future generations experience American liberty reserved for those of goodwill.

There are no coincidences.
It is not by accident that you have this book.

All things have their season, and in their times all things pass under heaven.

A time to be born and a time to die.

A time to plant,
and a time to pluck up that which is planted.

A time to kill, and a time to heal.

A time to destroy, and a time to build.

A time to weep, and a time to laugh.

A time to mourn, and a time to dance . . .[1]

Contents

Author's Note xi
Chronology. xiii
Introduction 1

PART I: In the Beginning 9
   Chapter 1: JFK's Early Years 11
   Chapter 2: Ideals. 35
   Chapter 3: Politics That Prevent War. 53

PART II: Freedom's Cost. 73
   Chapter 4: Seeking the US Presidency. 75
   Chapter 5: Leadership. 91
   Chapter 6: From Crisis to Crisis 109

PART III: Freedom's Triumph. 127
   Chapter 7: Cuban Missile Crisis 129
   Chapter 8: The Invisible Hand of Fate. 143
   Chapter 9: The Hand of Fate Strikes 155

Appendix One. 175
Appendix Two. 181
Appendix Three. 183
Appendix Four 189
Acknowledgements 201
Selected Bibliography 203
Notes 209

Author's Note

Great crises produce great men, and great deeds of courage.[2]
—John F. Kennedy

John F. Kennedy's patriotism is his greatest legacy. Three significant realities in his life propelled him to global immortality. First, he was born into a recently prosperous Christian family of Irish Catholic descent in Boston, Massachusetts at a time in American history when elites considered immigrant Irish Catholics as socially inferior. Secondly, John Fitzgerald Kennedy used the opportunities life presented him to feed the hungry, care for the imprisoned, visit the sick, bury the dead, admonish the fearful, instruct the ignorant, counsel the weak, forgive his enemies, serve the less fortunate, pray and sacrifice for everyone of all times and places. Thirdly, he never allowed fear or pain or failure to deter him.

As you examine the evidence in this small book, treasure Kennedy's life experiences that allow his heroic patriotism to shine through the prism of time. You will find that for Kennedy, a practicing Roman Catholic Christian who died a political, social, or perhaps even a religious martyr, patriotism meant personal sacrifice coupled with humble commitment to the great God of Abraham whom he worshipped to the best of his ability as Our Father Who art in Heaven. John F. Kennedy, true to his immigrant Irish heritage, was a follower of Jesus Christ through Mary from his birth in Boston to his public slaughter in Dallas, Texas that was witnessed around the world through the lens of television.

THE SPIRITUAL LEGACY OF JOHN F. KENNEDY

John F. Kennedy expressed his ancient Roman Catholic Christian faith tradition through personal heroism most especially within his family, nation, and the world at a time when Soviet hardliners of the day postured for first strike nuclear annihilation of vast swaths of the earth and its entire population. After you weigh the following testimony, some of which is in John Kennedy's own words uttered in significant speeches, and savor examples of his choices in the framework of his situated life opportunities as he faced personal and global crises, take the next step. Decide. Go forth and use this information as inspiration to make your own life and personal sphere of influence better for everyone. There are no lost opportunities. You will find that all humans make choices that have significant consequences not only for themselves but also for those they knowingly or unwittingly impact.[3]

This small work belongs to history. It contains memories of people who anonymously shared their personal experiences and recollections of America's thirty-fifth President, hoping to be heard, along with some of history's finest biographers. John F. Kennedy learned through heaven-permitted suffering and global responsibility that faith strengthened with hope enables people to lovingly serve others for the greater good of all. Ultimately, assassinated John F. Kennedy was a Roman Catholic whose Christian faith, hope and love were nurtured for Jesus Christ in the cradle of the Immaculate Heart of Mary on behalf of humankind.

Chronology

May 29, 1917: birth of John Fitzgerald Kennedy at family home in Brookline, a suburb of Boston, Massachusetts.

1927: the Kennedy family moves from Massachusetts to New York. JFK attends Riverdale Country Day School and, later, is sent to the Canterbury School in New Milford, Connecticut as a boarder.

1931: JFK transfers to the Choate boarding school in Wallingford, Connecticut where his older brother Joseph P. Kennedy Jr. is also enrolled.

1935-1936: JFK travels to England to study under Professor Harold Laski, becomes mortally ill and returns to hospital in Boston. JFK convalesces at family home in Palm Beach and later in Arizona.

1936: JFK enrolls at Harvard University.

1937: JFK joins the Harvard football, golf, and swim teams, and participates in thespian activities.

1938: second year at Harvard University. Fall term JFK plays football on the junior varsity team, swims on the varsity team, and joins the Spee and Yacht Clubs. He also works on the university newspaper, *The Harvard Crimson*. During summer break, he and a prep-school friend tour Europe on the eve of World War II. JFK recognizes what happens in Europe impacts the United States. JFK's knowledge differs from his isolationist father's opinion and that of his older brother, also a Harvard student.

1939: JFK obtains a leave of absence from Harvard to return to Europe, now on the brink of war. In England, where his father serves as US Ambassador, JFK steeps himself in the international diplomacy of the day.

1940: JFK graduates from Harvard University *magna cum laude* and publishes his first government book titled *Why England Slept*, which sells 80,000 copies worldwide. English royalties are donated to the English town of Plymouth which had been heavily bombed by German Nazis. He uses his American royalties to purchase a Buick convertible which he enjoys at Stanford University Graduate School of Business in Palo Alto, California while studying international business. JFK's draft deferral expires at the conclusion of his Stanford studies. Kennedy is declared unfit to serve (deemed 4-F) in the army and fails the required physical examination to become a naval officer.

1941: JFK accompanies his mother and younger sister Eunice on a Latin American tour of Argentina, Uruguay, Brazil, Chile, Ecuador, Peru, Columbia and Panama. After the

CHRONOLOGY

eight-country journey, JFK's father arranges for him to join the military in the Foreign Intelligence Office of Naval Intelligence, Washington, DC.

1942: JFK enrolls in midshipman's school at Northwestern University in Chicago.

1943: JFK takes command of a patrol-torpedo boat, the *PT-109*, serves seventeen months on a combat mission in the South Pacific war theater. During a nighttime mission to destroy a Japanese convoy, his wooden-hull *PT-109* is hit broadside by an enemy ship in raging seas. Two crew members are killed, the others, some injured, are cast adrift in mine- and shark-infested seas. JFK courageously helps his traumatized crew swim for approximately five hours to the nearest island. His extraordinary, innate bravery and unspoken heroism allow him to save his remaining crew members at great personal physical cost. John F. Kennedy is subsequently awarded the Navy and Marine Medal along with the Purple Heart Medal.

1944: JFK undergoes major back surgery trying to correct war injuries.

1947-1953: JFK serves as US Congressman for Massachusetts.

!953-1960: JFK serves as US Senator for Massachusetts.

1953: John F. Kennedy weds Jacqueline Lee Bouvier.

1955: mortally ill JFK undergoes two major back surgeries.

1956: convalescing JFK writes second book, Pulitzer Prize-winning, *Profiles in Courage*.

1960: JFK is elected thirty-fifth president of the United States of America.

1963: JFK is assassinated in Dallas, Texas.

INTRODUCTION

The Invisible Hand of Fate

The woods are lovely, dark and deep.
But I have promises to keep,
And miles to go before I sleep.
—Robert Frost

Frontiersmen and women, in spite of suffering and obstacles, are driven by unseen forces that propel them ever onward as they conquer the stark wilderness of their times and places. Each subsequent generation is influenced by the invisible hand of fate that guides them.

American history is a comfort, for it teaches that everyone's "higher power" worldwide was presciently identified by the ultimate frontiersman, America's first and only unanimously elected President, George Washington, as a "Kind Providence." John F. Kennedy resonated with George Washington's Kind Providence whom he knew and worshipped as Jesus Christ, only begotten Son of the Eternal Father who was born of the Blessed Virgin Mary. Kennedy, like George Washington, believed Christ brings light out of darkness, strength out of weakness, and resurrection out of death. He recognized early in life that eventually, we all surrender to the Lord's invisible hand of fate, the Lord who knows us better than we know ourselves, knows our world, its complications, sorrows and mysteries, and all our flawed hearts' desires but loves us unconditionally anyway, and guides us, perhaps simply because we are all needy humans dependent on fate's saving hand.

The thirty-fifth president of the United States, John F. Kennedy, is now locked in the pages of American history. He was a man so unique that few peers recognized the Lord's mysterious hand of fate that shielded him from the brightest limelight of his times. Kennedy managed, in spite of many personal physical weaknesses, to contribute powerfully to humanity in ways few understand but every generation must admire. No one disputes that Kennedy knew George Washington's "All Wise and Most Gracious Providence" well. Like US First President, General George Washington, JFK too believed the Gates of Paradise are opened by the "Blood of the Lamb" that has obtained entry for all the redeemed.[4] John Kennedy, like George Washington, did hand-to-hand combat with malevolent forces, but he did not pull back in fear or pain. Born into Boston's fundamentally Protestant Christian culture, Kennedy nobly carried the scars of the ancient Church of Rome so effectively that his charisma opened the fierce door of prejudice wide, allowing the brilliant sunlight of Christianity in its fullness to dissolve cobwebs of despair that had spawned revolutions and destroyed nations and families.

American history can be a profound comfort when it teaches that Jesus Christ, however the visible presence of the Creator is fathomed, brings good out of evil.[5] Some call this divine action a "terrible grace,"⁶ or perhaps even mysterious divine mercy that transcends human understanding.⁷ John F. Kennedy knew, honored, and served Jesus Christ whom he worshipped through the spiritual lens of his Catholic Christian heritage, his devout parents, siblings, unique life experiences, elite education, World War II US Navy service, British, European, Latin American and Asian diplomatic training, global colleagues, political successes and failures, sicknesses and injuries, marriage, parenthood, US Congressional and Presidential leadership. Like his hero George Washington, JFK, youngest and most narrowly elected US President, recognized that every man and his fate rise and fall on every choice he makes.⁸

Jack Kennedy was not a stranger to pain, sickness, sorrow, hunger, thirst, persecution, betrayal, violence, war, terrorism, and finally, assassination. Kennedy bequeathed his many accomplishments to successive generations throughout the world, but his physical weaknesses fade into dust.⁹ JFK's greatness rests in his singular ability to face misfortune and conquer it.¹⁰ He achieved victory where many others similarly situated failed through his highly tested faith in Divine Providence, his deep trust in George Washington's "All Knowing Benevolence," and his dogged human perseverance. JFK's tools were extreme personal discipline refined in the silence of his interior prayer life, commitment, and the graced ability to use every opportunity life presented to bend his will under the yoke of the Divine Will's illuminating ways recorded in scripture, tradition, history, family, and twentieth-century culture.

In her autobiography, John F. Kennedy's octogenarian mother Rose Fitzgerald Kennedy mused that "millions and millions of words" have already been written about her family but she lamented "most of it has, at best, been flawed in inaccuracies, misunderstandings, misinterpretations, and the worst has been mendacious and deceitful or even totally untrue stories that sound like pulp fiction and are often confused with history."[11] Taking to heart the concerns of John F. Kennedy's remarkable mother, this small work adds more words to the Kennedy love stories that saved the earth's population from nuclear destruction. Although scholars continue to plough through the millions of written words about John Kennedy bequeathed to poor players on life's ever-expanding stage, this small work strives to focus on the spiritual legacy of the thirty-fifth US President while political currents swirl about as global technology connects everyone everywhere.

Rose and Joe Kennedy's sickly, second-born son, John, against all odds, became the thirty-fifth President of the US. Before JFK lived and died as a resident of the White House on Pennsylvania Avenue, his lovely, mysteriously beautiful wife Jacqueline and he, their tiny daughter Caroline, and her nurse Miss Shaw lived a few houses east of Wisconsin Avenue in Georgetown on N Street when JFK was simply the junior senator from Massachusetts. It was reasonably well known that Senator John F. Kennedy often walked alone from his N Street residence to Sunday Mass at Holy Trinity parish church in Georgetown. In those times, he required no security detail. It was well known that Kennedy never missed Sunday Mass. It was also reasonably well known that he stood in line to confess on Saturdays. None could possibly fathom that the stalwart-looking Massachusetts junior senator could be sickly.

THE INVISIBLE HAND OF FATE

The jovial senator, whose mother was a Papal Countess, occasionally seemed to enjoy talking with others along the way to Georgetown's Holy Trinity parish church.[12] In autumn of 1959, a few N Street neighbors who were students at Georgetown University School of Foreign Service were not surprised as cheerful JFK reached into his suit pocket and pulled out his rosary beads while he encouraged them to complain less about the complexities of their classes and pray more, especially at exam time. On a warm, sunny Georgetown morning in 1959, it seemed inconceivable that three years later, in October of 1962, the invisible hand of fate would choose the rosary-carrying President of the United States, John F. Kennedy to delay Armageddon. Even more shocking would be his widely prophesied assassination a year later.

The thousand days of JFK's United States presidential leadership were intellectually fortified not only with his deep Catholic Christian faith; they were heavily infused with all his life experiences.[13] Arthur M. Schlesinger, Jr. a notable Harvard historian who served with JFK in the White House admitted that he struggled to describe Kennedy's inexplicable character when he mused: "He [Kennedy] was pragmatic in the sense that he tested the meaning of a proposition by its consequences, but he was also pragmatic in the sense of being free of metaphysics."[14] Schlesinger acknowledged that he struggled to categorize the overall presidency of John F. Kennedy, but concluded that JFK's leadership was not steeped in narrow ideology.[15]

History affirms that JFK's global governmental vision was unparalleled at the time. The Lord's invisible hand of fate shining through Kennedy's patriotic love story sparked the imaginations of post-World War II American voters, especially those who were television viewers in the second half of the last century. Historically a man ontologically ahead of his times, JFK brought enigmatic luminosity into some of his presidential decisions. More than six decades later, fate's invisible hand continues mysteriously to intrigue, fascinate, and prick the consciences of thinking people everywhere who ponder John F. Kennedy's extraordinary leadership as he and his Russian counterpart Nikita Khruschev heroically delayed the deadly consequences of nuclear Armageddon.

Years ago, a young medical student announced forthrightly: "JFK could not have been a philanderer. He was so medically compromised that he was lucky he had children."[16] Though Kennedy was physically impaired, he was spiritually deep. When the thirty-fifth US President was assassinated, his widow, Jacqueline Bouvier Kennedy's soul-wrenching agony was beamed to the world through the lens of television. The tears of the sorrowful mother clinging to her two tiny, fatherless children, Caroline and John Jr., validated John F. Kennedy's faithfulness not only to them, but ominously, to every subsequent American generation. There would be no human population on earth today but for JFK's numinous acuity in late November of 1962. When America faced off geopolitically with Soviet Russia during the Cuban missile crisis, nuclear Armageddon was averted. Life went on.

Moderns continue to underappreciate the diabolic power of global nuclear confrontation. Truth, however, gently unfolds as history progresses. With the lens of twenty-first century technology, consider the value of each person alive today. If science is correct, but for the graces that mysteriously flowed to and from Jack Kennedy, and his counterpart, Nikita Khruschev, this earth would be a nuclear wasteland. JFK's spiritual legacy challenges everyone of good will in all times and places: "Those who foolishly seek power by riding the back of the tiger end up inside . . . What can we do for the freedom of all humankind?"[17]

PART 1

In the Beginning

There is a spark of goodness in everyone.
—Lucia Dos Santos

The winds of Divine Providence drove immigrants from all across Ireland to Boston's shores in the mid-1850s when disaster afflicted their homeland on the Emerald Isle.[18] Among them were the penniless ancestors of John F. Kennedy, who would become the youngest and most the narrowly elected President of the United States, a hundred years later.

ONE

JFK's Early Years

*"Ask not what your country can do for you—
ask what you can do for your country."*
—John Kennedy Inaugural Address

JFK's parents Rose and Joe Kennedy, third generation descendants of Irish Catholic Christian immigrants, were sweethearts for seven years before marriage. They had met as small children and later admitted that they each knew, even then, that they were destined for one another. Rose Fitzgerald was the daughter of Boston's flamboyant Irish Catholic Christian mayor, John Fitzgerald, whose parents had died at a young age, leaving him to care for his six brothers by giving up his place at Harvard Medical School.

Mayor Fitzgerald, popularly known as Honey Fitz, did all he could to dissuade his beautiful, diminutive eldest daughter, Rose, with her twinkling blue eyes, quick smile, and dark, naturally curly hair from seeing the tall, thin, quick-witted Joe Kennedy, son of Harvard educated Patrick J. Kennedy, a local banker and minor politician known as P. J. Honey Fitz even arranged for his petite Rose and her younger sister Agnes to spend a year abroad at an austere, all-girls cloistered Convent of the Sacred Heart in Holland where they would study and learn ideal Catholic Christian homemaking skills with daughters of European aristocracy of similar ages. His hope was that his Rose would forget P. J. Kennedy's only son Joe as she struggled to adjust to convent life where "the nun's routine combined British boarding-school regimentation with Marine boot-camp discipline."[19]

Joseph Patrick Kennedy was born on September 6, 1888, in East Boston. He was the cherished, protected, only son of Patrick Joseph and Mary Josephine (Josie) Hickey Kennedy. Joe's father P. J. was a powerful, respected businessman and political ward leader. Joe was quite self-aware from a young age. He rightfully considered himself the smartest man around.[20] Young Joe studied at the prestigious Boston Latin School where he was a star baseball and basketball player, captain of the baseball and tennis teams, and senior class president before attending Harvard University, his father's *alma mater*. Few people ever really knew Joe Kennedy who rarely, if ever, allowed anyone personal closeness. Quietly religious and deeply driven, he recognized early in his life that he was naturally attracted to truth, goodness, and beauty. He was also aware that such ideals were expensive, but he was determined to acquire his heart's desires.

At Harvard, he studied economics and was a member of the Hasty Pudding Club and Delta Upsilon. Joe had "tremendous charm."[21] During his senior year of university he lived in Hollis Hall, Harvard's best dormitory. Professors and colleagues said Joe "led a model life at Harvard. He attended Mass every Sunday and was a First Friday communicant as well. He never drank, smoked, or gambled at cards—off color stories were taboo."[22] Joe never even drank coffee. He had none of the known collegiate vices. His dad, P. J., was Joe's hero, a man of "dignity, discretion and decency."[23]

P. J. and Joe had little political respect for Boston's mayor, Honey Fitz, whom some referred to as an "unscrupulous buffoon."[24] Joe had decided at an early age that he would follow the advice of Socrates, an ancient Greek savant who was critical of tribalism and factionalism in politics, which he believed produced close-knit camps of warring enemies. Socrates said a man who sincerely fights for justice must lead a private, not a public life. P. J.'s only son would adhere to Socratic wisdom during his entire life. Unfortunately, wherever a vacuum exists, darkness tends to envelop it.

Upon graduation, Joe passed the civil service examination for assistant bank examiners. Though the job paid little, $1,500 per year, it provided hands-on, inside knowledge of the inner workings of banking and allowed Joe to meet significant trustees and directors of the largest banks in Massachusetts. In this capacity, dedicated, assiduous Joe Kennedy learned invaluable financial information about stocks, and bonds, mortgages, demand loans, collateralized time loans, overdrafts, foreclosed real estate, currencies and specie.[25] Once Joe had acquired sufficient knowledge of the inner workings of banking that grease the wheels of fortune, he moved on to consolidate his position as president of the Columbia Trust Bank, of which his dad was a director. This career decision made twenty-five-year-old Joe Kennedy the youngest bank president in the United States.

The heart has ways that the head does not know.[26] Notwithstanding the very best efforts of Honey Fitz, his daughter

Rose and P. J.'s son Joe were destined for each other. Distance only seemed to fan the flames of Joe Kennedy's fascination with Rose Fitzgerald and the brilliant spiritual charms she hid deep in her soul that she shared only with him. Rose remained captivated with Joe's profound spirituality, which he effectively hid from everyone but her, along with his windblown blond hair tinged with red highlights, his easy grin, his freckles, his interior and athletic strengths, and perhaps most of all, his undeniable dedication to her during his entire life.

Finally, Honey Fitz relented in his efforts to choose a spouse for his headstrong little Rose and welcomed Joe Kennedy as his mysteriously brilliant, but seriously complicated son-in-law. The winds of Divine Providence sometimes shelter poor players who strut and fret upon earth's surface striving, always striving to find purpose and harmony with powerful currents few even recognize. Rose and Joe Kennedy would enjoy a long and fruitful sacramental marriage; the fulfillment of a unique divine grace they had intuited from the first moment they met. Few penetrate the depths of their exquisite, rare, personal relationship.

Rose knew unequivocally that Joe would remain faithful to her the way sincere Christian men of his generation and class remained faithful to their wives. Joe was certain that as long as he protected, cherished, and provided generously for his Rose and their nine children, she would always be there for him. He wanted nothing more. The lens of history, however, continues to analyze the effects of their marriage, not only through their personal, respective accomplishments, but also the actions of their children whom they faithfully raised, not for their own satisfaction, but for the glory of Divine Providence as they understood their immortal duties.

Rose and Joe Kennedy's sacramental wedding was small, attended only by close family members. Joe purchased a family home for Rose and himself that had a gabled roof and a large balustraded porch. Rose, used to the best, immediately employed a fashionable interior designer to arrange their home's lovely furnishings around a grand piano she had received from her paternal uncles as a wedding gift. Rose and Joe both believed that a grand piano could be the heart of their home where beauty and peace were desired. Rose played her piano every day, certain that Joe, who had no gift for music, would find relaxation and peace as he listened. Their shared hope was that, like prior family generations, they would soon have many of their own children to share their joy. The young couple began their lives together honeymooning at the Greenbriar Resort in White Sulphur Springs, West Virginia, which was renowned for its refinement, tasteful décor, fine food, and healing spa.

Just as the United States entered World War I, their second son John F. Kennedy was born at his parents' home on Beale Street in Brookline, a suburb of Boston, on May 29, 1917. JFK's mother, who treasured being the beloved eldest daughter of Boston's retired mayor, and her beautiful, refined but humble mother, Mary Hannon Fitzgerald, was delighted that her parents lived nearby. Rose's devout Irish Catholic Christian parents' joy, especially Mayor Fitzgerald's, was palpable when they learned that the second son of their cherished twenty-six-year-old daughter Rose would be named for him; John Fitzgerald Kennedy. They could not know the extraordinary hand of fate that hovered over the shivering newborn boy whom everyone would call Jack.

Young bank president of local Columbia Trust, Joseph P. Kennedy, had an appointment with his own destiny on the birth day of his second son, but he was not present for the birth. The custom of the day was that birthing was a woman's job. Joe Kennedy was duly elected to the Massachusetts Electric Company on that fateful day. He was twenty-eight years old. JFK's older brother Joe Jr. was two years old when he met his newborn brother.

Joe Senior had known during his student days at Harvard, and long before he graduated in 1912, that his future was in business and finance. From early childhood, he recognized that the source and stability of business was money, and banking controlled the money flow in the United States and abroad. Joe wanted to know the financial rules by which he must abide and to do so, he needed access to the source of the money that facilitated commerce and industry. His father P. J. was one of the original founders of the local Columbia Trust Bank which served the small business interests of East Boston.[27] He would provide an opening in that bank for his only son.[28]

It was well known that outspoken Joe Kennedy, now a proud father of two sons, abhorred war. He saw it as senseless slaughter of the best and brightest of the times. Many of his fellow Harvard peers disagreed with him and some had volunteered to serve in the European conflict. When the US entered World War I, Joe knew that he had to find a way to avoid conscription as deadly European hostilities spread across the globe. US military conscription, known as the draft, was enforced by the federal government during six international conflicts: the Revolutionary War, the Civil War, World War I, World War II, the Korean War, and the Vietnam War. Conscription remains in place today on a contingency basis for all US male citizens, regardless of where they reside, and for all male immigrants both documented and undocumented residing within the United States who are age eighteen through twenty-five. All men are required to register with the Selective Service System. Failure to register can trigger denial of federal services including health care. Article 1, Section 8 of the US Constitution and 10 US Code 246 permit compulsory conscription of men between the ages of seventeen and forty-four who are, or who have made a declaration of intention to become US citizens, and women in certain health care occupations for military service.

The US Congress approved a resolution to declare war on Germany on April 6, 1917. President Woodrow Wilson requested the resolution when Germany engaged in submarine warfare against US merchant ships in the Atlantic and Mediterranean seas. Enjoying a bit of the luck of the Irish, by September of 1917, Joe changed jobs, becoming assistant general manager of Bethlehem Steel's Fore River shipbuilding plant in nearby Quincy.[29] This job, paying $4,000 per year, would provide Joe with an industrial exemption from the draft.[30] He knew steel was vital to the US war effort in Europe. Joe was delighted that his employment at this unique, multimillion-dollar steel operation effectively gave him personal access to major decision-makers in Washington, DC and abroad. His dearly esteemed wife Rose had been raised with fine taste, but her health was far from stalwart. Aware that his father-in-law held him to the highest standards, Joe would do his utmost to honor his wedding vows by providing for Rose and their children in the best possible financial ways of the times. His own work ethic was so admirable that when the First World War ended, Charles M. Schwab, President of Bethlehem Steel Corporation sought him out to personally thank him for his remarkable service. Joe could not know then that a pattern was being established for his little family that would impact the entire world.

After two years of grueling, round the clock work at the shipbuilding plant that left him physically sick and even more war-weary, Joe made another strategic career change. Now savvy about lucrative government contracts and contacts, Joe accepted a managerial position with the prominent Boston stock brokerage firm of Haydon, Stone, and Company where he remained for six years. He had met Gaylon Stone during his Fore River days. Stone, who would become Joe's mentor, was co-owner of the brokerage firm that had influential offices in Boston and New York. During the years Joe Kennedy managed the brokerage department of Haydon Stone, he continued to acquire real estate investments on the side. In those times, astute Joe Kennedy amassed a fortune of two million dollars.[31] Through Columbia Trust and his Harvard contacts who worked in banking, Joe Kennedy had obtained working capital to fund his varied investments.[32]

After the stock market crash of 1929, financial regulations within the brokerage industry were necessary to ensure orderly markets at home and abroad. By 1934, President Franklin D. Roosevelt appointed Joe Kennedy chairman of the newly formed

Securities and Exchange Commission, which enforces the regulations of the Federal Security Exchange laws. Joe dutifully drafted rules to restore investor confidence in financial markets by outlawing fraud, prohibiting insider trading, requiring registration of securities exchanges, and over-the-counter markets operating in interstate and foreign commerce, and through the mails. The Securities Exchange Act of 1934 continues to regulate secondary financial markets by requiring a transparent and fair market environment for investors, prohibition of insider trading, and disclosure of important information to current and potential shareholders by publicly traded companies.

Known professionally as a family man, devout Christian (Catholic denomination), Harvard alumnus, and Mayor Honey Fitz's son-in-law, Joe Kennedy became more or less respected in wider and more influential financial circles. Scandal was not associated with him or his growing family. Astute Joe Kennedy knew the financial regulations of his times and was most careful to stay within their parameters. History discloses that JFK's father was not, nor was he ever a highly maligned bootlegger. Eminent biographer David Nasaw discovered after extensive research that Jospeh Kennedy Senior ". . . was willing to take financial risks, but not those associated with illegal activities such as bootlegging."[33]

By the time young Jack was six years old in 1923, his father opened his own stock brokerage firm on a different floor of the same building where Haydon Stone was located. His goal was to increase his personal fortune. In 1927, when Jack was ten years old, Joe Senior moved his family to a New York suburb so that he could be closer to his work on Wall Street. Rose missed

Boston and was terribly lonely not only for her family, but also for her friends and her hometown.

By 1933, when Prohibition was repealed, Joe Kennedy was well positioned to prosper even more. He went into the highly lucrative, legitimate alcohol industry by garnering exclusive US import and distribution licenses for Haig and Haig and Dewars Scotch whiskies, and Gordon's Gin. To keep the family's Boston roots and be near family, Rose and Joe rented a seaside home in Hyannis Port which they eventually were able to purchase. Joe effectively organized his business associations so that he too could summer with his growing family at Hyannis Port. Joe insisted upon competitive sports among the siblings while Rose kept the family properly nourished and clothed. Joe especially liked dinner meals during which he thoroughly enjoyed his esteemed place at the head of the table where he could guide and manage the intellectual development of his gifted family.

While Joe was busy amassing a family fortune that created a flame to light the way for his wife and children to dedicate their lives to helping the less fortunate, Rose too was busy at home enduring the travails and experiencing the joys of motherhood. Rosemary was born a year after JFK, during the era of the Spanish Flu pandemic that vanquished fifty million people worldwide. This child named for her mother Rose, and the Blessed Virgin Mary, had developmental issues that would one day prove a blessing for many similarly situated children and adults. Though Rosemary's condition was a particularly difficult problem for Rose and Joe at a historical time when mentally challenged children were rarely mainstreamed, her eight deeply compassionate siblings would share their love for her by founding government-funded programs such as the Peace Corps and the Special Olympics; both are dedicated to improving the lives of needy others.

Rose said of herself: "My great ambition was to have my children morally, physically, and mentally as perfect as possible."[34] Joe concurred with this noble ambition to the best of his ability to understand it. As the years unfolded, Rose and Joe had no choice but to accept that perfection, as humans perceive it, is not yet of this world. Rose, however, never doubted that God's infinite love for everyone throughout the world is perfect for purposes of this earthy life.[35] Rose succeeded in imparting her trust in the perfect love of God for all His dearly redeemed people in very differing ways into each of her nine children.[36] Her faith was tested severely, but she persevered and prevailed as her long, long life unfolded.[37] The nine Kennedy children were able to love and help one another as few others of their times.[38]

Two- and one-half year-old JFK welcomed another baby sister named Kathleen who would later open the door of her Irish Catholic Christian family to the graciousness of ecumenical love when she married into Anglican Catholic Christian aristocracy. JFK's tiny sister Eunice, who would share the affliction of Addison's disease with him, was born a year after Kathleen. Patricia arrived when Jack was seven, and a year later, his brother Robert, familiarly known as Bobby, was born. His sister Jean arrived when JFK was nine and his youngest sibling, Edward, always called Teddy, was born when Jack was thirteen. Jack personally asked his mom to allow him to be Teddy's godfather, which he was.

In his formative years, JFK learned that his strict, demanding father was always busy providing for his growing family, and away much of the time. His mother Rose, who before her marriage had traveled extensively with her father when he was mayor of Boston, was highly dedicated to her ancient Catholic faith traditions. Although Rose's mother Mary Josephine, known as Josie, was an affable introvert, Rose had a self-contained personality: she enjoyed sitting alone quietly and reading or even traveling alone. But Rose was also completely at ease before crowds, perhaps due to the influence of her highly extraverted father, the inveterate Boston mayor and perpetual politician Honey Fitz.[39] To Joe's challenging delight, Rose bore him nine needy infants before JFK became a teenager. All of them reached adulthood at a historical time when many infants did not survive childhood.[40] As young Jack grew up, his mother would again become a world traveler, but like his dad, he quickly recognized that his mom was "the glue that held the family together."[41]

Childhood and teen years were somewhat difficult and quite challenging for young Jack Kennedy. He was thin, asthmatic, and sickly, probably having both undiagnosed Celiac's and Addison's diseases. As a toddler, with his compromised immune system, he had suffered scarlet fever which was a highly contagious disease at the time that spread rapidly and was more often than not fatal. One of the effects that was little known at the time was permanent weakening of the heart valves. In the early part of the twentieth century, before antibiotics, the mortality rate from scarlet fever in the US reached 25 percent.

Because of the likelihood of contagion for his other vulnerable siblings, two-and-a-half-year-old Jack, terribly sick with scarlet fever, was sent to Boston City Hospital. During that interim, because nursing mother Rose was recovering from childbirth, Joe Senior undertook care of his perilously sick second son. For two months, Joe rose early each day to attend morning Mass, worshipping for tiny Jack. When JFK became even sicker, his distraught dad made a deal with God, promising to donate half his fortune to the needy if his tiny second son would be spared. After early morning Mass, Joe went to work at Haydon Stone. At midafternoon, when the financial markets closed for the day, Joe returned to Boston City Hospital where he prayed fervently by the bedside of his mortally sick little boy. Slowly, toddler Jack began to improve. Joe believed that through Christ, his best-efforts prayer is continuous and contagious.[42] Inexplicably, extremely sick little Jack knew his mom and dad and grandparents and uncles and aunts were enveloping him in prayer and he joined them with his baby prayers too.[43] Because clinical evidence indicated that scarlet fever contagion would remain for up to five months, Jack was sent to Mansion House in Poland Springs, Maine with a full-time nurse to complete his convalescence before he was allowed to come home.

During that time, Rose was somewhat reassured that her tiny Jack was cherished by his medical caregivers who said he was a true delight. Rose, the nursing mother of newborn Kathleen, was forced by circumstances beyond her control to prayerfully accept that childbearing and its accompanying malaise had separated her from her extremely sick little Jack whom she believed needed his mother. Her comfort rested in her devout husband's faith-filled strength that guided him to prayerfully overcome their family medical trauma.[44] No one else in the family fell victim to scarlet fever. Joe had been relentless in finding the best expertise the medical community of the times offered for children suffering from the dangerous scarlet fever bacterial Streptococcus pyogenes infection. He skillfully kept his critically ill second son from afflicting his vulnerable wife and tiny Jack's other highly vulnerable siblings. Astute Harvard alumnus Joe Kennedy personally followed the well-known teaching of soldier-saint Ignatius of Loyola; he prayed as if Jack's cure was all up to God and worked as if his tiny son's cure was all up to his efforts to obtain the best medical care available. Years later, Rose sadly revealed her ongoing concern that her little boy Jack needed her attention "perhaps more than I gave him in my worry and distraction . . . I sometimes wondered if he had felt neglected by me."[45]

Historically, when Christians recognize their powerlessness over circumstances, the New Testament teaches them to turn to Jesus, their acknowledged incarnate "higher power" who is all knowing, all powerful, and all loving. During Jack's childhood, he saw his mother (and occasionally his father) worship daily at morning Mass and afterward, remain at their parish church to prayerfully meditate upon the gospel mysteries of the rosary. Rose and Joe occasionally brought their sickly second son with them to their daily worship. Sunday Mass was a family gathering with the Lord that was often followed by visits to grandparents when they lived in the same city. Every day, faithful to contemporary pediatric principles, Rose and Joe required outdoor activities for their growing children in spite of the challenging New England weather. Their favorite outdoor activities were centered around daily walks to their parish church where they were taught to worship Jesus sacramentally present there in a tabernacle on the high altar. The children learned they could find solace by confiding in sacramental Jesus their frustrations, dreams, goals, and longings. As their faith grew, so also did their trust in Christ's power to bring good out of evil.[46] After their daily visit with Jesus, Rose and her children walked to a nearby market for a treat, and weather permitting, finished their outing with a visit to a nearby patriotic memorial recognizing one of Boston's early revolutionary war heroes.

Many heard Rose explain in her later years that her religious beliefs were her sustenance and survival throughout her long, difficult, and fruitful life. She expressed her confidence that her husband and children shared her beliefs. Little could she and Joe know how their mysteriously humble, sacrificially lived-out Christian beliefs would sustain and guide world decision-makers in peace and war.[47]

As religiously strict with herself and deeply conservative as was Rose, her beloved spouse, Joe Senior had a more adventurous spirit. His thought process was innovative and wide-ranging. His aptitude for amassing wealth manifested in his university days and continued throughout his productive professional life. Enduring trials that would destroy most couples, Rose and Joe had a unique and satisfying love story that they nurtured and protected in sickness and in health throughout their lives.[48]

Realistic Joe was perceptively aware of the absolute necessity of money to survive and thrive in American life of his times. Biographer David Nasaw observed: "In marrying Rose Fitzgerald, Joe Kennedy had pledged to faithfully love and support her—and the children they might have together, to keep them safe and secure and well sheltered, and to do everything in his power, to work day and night, six days a week, fifty-two weeks a year if necessary, to provide for them."[49] He was brilliantly faithful to that commitment, and often in ways only he and Rose knew. Joe Kennedy's financial acumen of course greatly benefitted not only his immediate family, but also people of diverse backgrounds and nations who would work in his household, offices, professional, social, motion picture, and diplomatic services. Rose was religiously and educationally strong enough to be a fitting spouse for a man with the global destiny of Joseph P. Kennedy. For his part, Joe was intelligent and loving enough to protect his wife from difficulties that he believed would unnecessarily wound her.

Both Joe and Rose were aware of their sacramental marital commitments. They recognized that they were not meant to be spiritually apart. Unfortunately, as world economic realities changed, Joe's business expertise led him to absences from his wife, children, and family. Both he and Rose believed that God's grace flows through and between spouses. They understood that the Lord comes in and with the sacrament of matrimony whenever spouses are together because God is present in a sacramental presence. Joe telephoned Rose nearly every day no matter where he was or what he was doing.

Joe and Rose recognized that God made a sacramental covenant between spouses. To separate spouses is to violate and abrogate God's covenant. People do this at their own spiritual peril. The immutable spiritual law teaches clearly that sacramentally married people may never choose any action in life that excludes their spouse. Both Rose and Joe were careful with this imperative, which required Joe to be solicitous about protecting his beloved Rose's often fragile health. Rose and Joe were each thoroughly committed to their mutual duty to lead one another to the Heavenly Kingdom. Through their sacramental bond, the divine blessing flowed through them to their offspring.

A simple test for God's sacred Plan (as opposed to one sourced in either spouse's ego) is how well any situation or opportunity serves each spouse in a marriage. Wherever exploitation exists, the evil one gains. God's sacred Plan never includes exploitation of any of His dearly redeemed children. God's sacred Plan in sacramental marriage is that the bride and groom become one flesh. Then ego dies and love flourishes. Selfishness in marriage leads to evil because it drives God away. When God departs, His grace and protection depart.

Where spouses work together, pray together, and play together, God is present in a sacramental bond. The two do become one. As Christ laid down His life out of love for His Father's sacred Plan, so spouses lay down their lives for one another in fulfillment of their part in the sacred Plan. The humblest work of spouses together is more beautiful in Paradise than the noblest work of a spouse done alone for self, apart from the sacramental bond of matrimony.

Among the ever-growing brood of young Kennedy children, Jack's older brother Joe Jr. was a mixed blessing. Always confident, highly intelligent, a fine athlete, handsome and strong, he deeply loved his little brothers and sisters and delighted in their company. Close to both his mom and dad, Joe was taught at a young age to shepherd his younger siblings with love. He enjoyed motivating Jack, encouraging him to strive for excellence. Joe Jr. had unassailable courage and imparted that virtue to Jack, most especially whenever the sickly, struggling little boy obviously labored to keep up with his older brother. Young Jack idolized Joe Jr. but was never intimidated by him. He deeply admired his older brother and did his best to match Joe's formidable skills. Because his father, striving to become a scion of Wall Street, and in the lucrative motion picture business in Hollywood, was away frequently, Joe Jr. effectively became Jack's cherished male hero and role model. Joe Senior, however, stayed in close contact with both Joe Jr. and Jack as he and Rose monitored their growing family with loving, sacrificial devotion.

Like most of his affluent peers in Bronxville, New York, where the family had relocated, Joe Jr. was sent to boarding school at Choate for his high school years. His absence was a great loss to Jack who had become his older brother's shadow. Though he was still quite young, Rose and Joe Senior, hoping to help him, sent lonely, sickly JFK to a strict, all boys Catholic boarding school in nearby Connecticut. Thirteen-year-old Jack was quite homesick and continued to miss his older brother Joe Jr. even more as he navigated alone through strange surroundings and austere regulations.

To Rose and Joe's delight, young Jack grew in his loyalty to Jesus by accepting his Christian duties through devotion to Christ aided by the intercession of His Mother Mary, especially during his stint at Canterbury.[50] During his many lonely days in Canterbury's infirmary, sickly John Fitzgerald Kennedy read about brilliant soldier saints such as Francis of Assisi, and Jesuit founder Ignatius of Loyola, along with miracles of Dominican saint and scholar Albertus Magnus who mentored the eminent Thomas Aquinas. JFK even learned about the apocalyptic warnings of French Saint Louis de Montfort who explained the signs of the latter days more than three hundred years ago.

> "In the second coming of Jesus Christ,
> Mary has to be made known and revealed
> by the Holy Spirit in order that, through
> her, Jesus Christ may be [correctly] known,
> loved and served."[51]

1929–1930 was a time of world-wide depression. During this financial debacle, young teenager JFK would remember how many out-of-work people his parents hired, simply so that their families could survive. The financial crisis, however, did not hurt the Kennedy family.

In his one year at Canterbury, young JFK endured a mysterious illness during which he lost a great deal of weight and experienced serious fatigue. Already suffering with undiagnosed Addison's disease, and as Celiac's disease was not readily recognized much less diagnosable at the time, modern medical experts suggest those were probably the underlying sources of JFK's many difficult teenage illnesses.[52] Such actual knowledge, however, remains quite unknowable.[53] Because he spent so much time in Canterbury's infirmary, the lonely young student remembered that he was told he had "special time" to pray. Of course, JFK was not pleased that his health was such a challenge but as his interior prayer life deepened, his health became even more of a mystery to him. In spring of 1931, Jack underwent an emergency appendectomy. When he attempted to excel in athletics, he suffered from knee difficulties as he tried to regain his strength in school sports. This condition was diagnosed as "growing pains" at the time. Now, however, teenage knee difficulty is frequently diagnosed as Osgood-Schlatter disease which happens during the growth spurt of puberty when human bones, muscles, and tendons grow at different rates. JFK would discover much later in life that his left leg was one inch shorter than his right leg and he would compensate with an orthopedic shoe lift.

In 1931, Jack began his own high school studies at Choate. Although the brothers were again in the same school, their relationship had changed. Jack Kennedy's health had become a serious issue for him and his concerned parents, but it was no better at Choate. Young Jack would hold the record for the most days spent in Choate's Archibald Infirmary. During his infirmary days, JFK read constantly. His parents made certain that their second son had the lives of the saints to ponder. Joe also supplied his eager young second son with thrilling adventure stories of great heroes who made vast differences in society through their courageous deeds. His parents did not tire of reminding Jack of graces he was receiving by offering his personal pain and disappointments in common with Jesus, the suffering servant Redeemer. They assured their sickly son that his ailments were a gift with eternal value. By age sixteen, Jack was so thin that some of his pals began to refer to him jokingly as "rat face." Joe Jr., who had by now moved on to his father and grandfather P. J.'s *alma mater,* Harvard University, continued to excel both on the athletic field and academically. Comparing himself to his older brother was a challenge for Jack who sincerely trusted his older brother.

JFK'S EARLY YEARS

Slowly, JFK blended into Choate's British boarding school mode. The teenager attended Mass on Sundays at the Catholic Church in Wallingford and continued what would become a lifetime habit, even during his three years in the White House, of kneeling beside his bed before retiring to say his nightly prayers that included an Our Father, Hail Mary, and Glory Be to the Father, Son, and Holy Spirit. Jack loved two sports in which, given his dedication to excellence, he excelled. Both golf and swimming were his choices, but the silence of sailing and the challenge of the winds and seas remained a favorite, too. Jack devoured the writings of Winston Churchill. He thrilled to the triumphs Churchill achieved and enjoyed the cynicism Churchill held for those who missed history's lessons.

Gradually, other interests than his health began to intrigue JFK. His world view came from his passion for reading and studying the lives of international leaders and influencers. Throughout his life, he continued to follow the pursuits of Winston Churchill. Jack's quick wit, charm and delicacy in appreciating the difficulties of others led his Choate peers to vote him the "Most Likely to Succeed" award. No one ever really had access to JFK's ever-growing interior life of familial intimacy with Jesus Christ through Mary.[54] During his entire life, those fortunate enough to be close to naturally reserved Jack Kennedy appreciated his capacity to care deeply about them, simply because he did.[55] Future generations have and will continue to ponder the mystery of John F. Kennedy. One example is American political commentator, retired talk show host, and author Chris Matthews who wrote: "My fascination with the elusive spirit of John F. Kennedy has remained an abiding one."[56] Life circumstances would hurl innumerable challenges all along the way of JFK's unique life and formation field. But his generation would learn, as serious historians of all times must, that John F. Kennedy as a world leader saved civilization from nuclear holocaust because he had become fully grounded in his faith, choices, and discernment.[57]

At seventeen, however, once again dangerously sick, JFK was sent by his distraught parents to the best medical facility of the day at Mayo Clinic in Rochester, Minnesota for what turned out to be gruesome diagnostic tests. The experience was brutal for the teenager. Medical "tests" at that time were a dreadful and embarrassing exercise in endurance. Although his dad visited him briefly at Mayo Clinic, Joe Senior would not permit Rose or his siblings to do so lest his mother "baby" him, or his siblings pity him. Later in life, JFK would realize that stalwart Joe Senior was determined to teach his sickly second son to appreciate, accept, and overcome hardship. After two weeks at the Mayo Clinic, seriously ill JFK was transferred to nearby Saint Mary's Hospital in Rochester. While a hospital inpatient, Jack experienced the graciousness and encouragement of a few Franciscan nuns who frequently visited and prayed with the lonely youth as he silently suffered the indignities of even more repugnant medical issues. During these trying medical experiences authorized by his concerned parents, Jack had painful times to pray and study and dream of heroes of yesteryear who had endured and conquered far worse experiences than his situation.

JFK, like all the Kennedy children, had been taught by his parents to "offer up in union with Jesus on the cross" not only every ache and pain, all disappointments and sorrows, but his very life for the glory of God and salvation of souls.[58] Rose and Joe consistently reassured their children that Jesus always brings good out of bad situations for those who remain faithful.[59] As difficult as that might have seemed to young Jack at Saint Mary's Hospital in Rochester, Minnesota, his focus changed. Now the suffering teenager had one goal: to get out of the hospital and move on with his life, whatever that might be.[60]

Introspective JFK suspected that he carried an undiagnosable illness that would continuously plague him, but he decided to make the best of what his earth sojourn offered. Of course, the nuns at St. Mary's Hospital were quick to remind him of the many blessings his parent's wealth provided for him. Young Jack would thereafter continue to do his best even though he naturally wondered whether he could ever measure up to his highly respected older brother Joe Jr. Infirmities have many faces and many mysterious purposes. As he approached adulthood, Jack Kennedy realized his medical situation provided him with unintended prayer, fasting, and abstinence as a way of life.[61]

TWO

Ideals

Blessed are the peacemakers
—Matthew 5:9

Jack and his sister Kathleen, born two-and-a half years apart, were extremely close, so close that many thought they were actually twins.[62] Of all the Kennedy children, Kathleen looked the most like her mother, Rose. Little Kathleen seemed "filled with [a] radiantly joyous, self-confident sense of life and youth."[63] Similarly suffering with asthma, Kathleen had deep, affectionate and loving compassion for her much-admired but sickly older brother Jack who also shared many physical characteristics of his mother. Rose, Kathleen, and second son Jack had dark hair, twinkling blue eyes and welcoming, affirming smiles that warmed the heart.

After his graduation from Choate in 1935, Jack and sixteen-year-old Kathleen sailed with their parents on the luxury ocean liner *Isle de France* to Europe where Joe Senior planned for Jack to study with world renown socialist Professor Harold Laski at the London School of Economics as Joe Jr. had done two years earlier. Rose planned for Kathleen to study in northeastern

France at a secluded Sacred Heart Convent where she hoped her lively daughter would absorb European culture and linguistic skills.[64]

Rose was authentic, disciplined, aesthetic but she also enjoyed the fine things of the world and respected the rules and rituals of her Catholic Christian faith tradition. She tried diligently to live a detachment that great saints teach. Her duty, as she understood it, was her gift to the Lord as she knew Him. Rose worshipped Jesus Christ daily at her parish Mass. She prayed and meditated on the mysteries of the rosary every day as she identified her travails with the path of Jesus and Mary as taught by the ancient Roman Catholic Christian denomination. Trained by her political father to be a woman beyond reproach, Rose abhorred scandal and took great effort to present the absolute best version of herself to the public. She faithfully bore nine children at a time when family planning for birth control was not integral to Catholic Christian life.

When Jack Kennedy was a year old, and Joe Jr. was three, Rose had borne a developmentally challenged daughter, Rosemary. Many wealthy parents of the time chose to hand off such children to professionals, who were better trained to provide suitable care and nurturing. This option was available only to the rich, for there was no governmental aid or social welfare to bear the costs. Rose and Joe Senior decided against institutionalizing Rosemary. Instead, they gently accepted her as a heavenly gift to their family, teaching her siblings likewise to love and care for her. When Rosemary became an adult, her dad sought the finest medical help in the world for his mentally impaired daughter, sincerely hoping to improve her quality of life and family participation. When the medical surgery was unsuccessful, Joe Senior found gracious housing and faith-filled caregivers who dedicated their lives to the spiritual and physical wellbeing of Rosemary Kennedy. Neither Joe Senior nor Rose ever complained about Rosemary. They did their best to provide a happy, fulfilling life for her. They taught her siblings to love Rosemary unconditionally and help her in every way possible.

    Joe Senior loved and admired his wife. He was overjoyed to have a large family. His authority was absolute in his home and Rose always deferred to him. Joe Senior was obviously a man ahead of his time in that he trusted Rose to manage his household with absolute authority. He abhorred disorder, was frugal in small matters, as was Rose, and accepted his responsibility to acquire the financial net worth that would provide not only stability, but opportunity for him and his family to make a significant contribution to society. Rose respected her husband and was delighted with his outstanding business acumen. She was ascetic by nature, choosing to rise early, swim in the cold Atlantic Ocean, as weather permitted, attend daily Mass, pray her rosary as she cared for her body, mind, and soul while nurturing her demanding husband, and ever-expanding brood of children. Rose carefully guided her household help, encouraging them to grow in diligence, thrift and refinement.

    Joe Senior was a business visionary. He saw opportunity for himself and his country that required effort most men would have abhorred, much less embraced. He was capable of hard work for long hours. Joe Senior was ascetic and dedicated to his church as he understood his duties, which he lived to the best of his ability. Rose respected his dedication to duty and encouraged him. Both Rose and Joe Senior grew in their respective family roles. They enjoyed having their parents live nearby and found inspiration in their presence. The Kennedy grandparents certainly enjoyed their grandchildren and saw them on a regular basis. Honey Fitz added flavor and conviviality to the Kennedy children with his quick wit and charm. He deeply admired his dear little Rose and encouraged her to expend immense effort to help Rosemary understand her unique value as a child of God destined to live forever in His Kingdom. He told the other children he expected them to be grateful they were not so needy.

While travelling to France with their parents, teenagers Kathleen and Jack enjoyed the ship's fine French flavor and most of all, the undivided attention of their parents during their ocean crossing. JFK had a wonderful sense of humor that he may have inherited from Honey Fitz, whose easy laugh laced with kindness had endeared him to voters, friends, and family. Even as a youngster, Jack had charm that Kathleen told him was rooted in divine grace. They had formed a sibling bond that would never end perhaps simply because they could not escape the tenderness they observed between their parents that mysteriously included them. Jack enjoyed telling Kathleen stories from books he had read about heroes who overcame hurdles the average man does not even see. She understood in ways that gave Jack comfort and reassurance.

During Jack's many hospital and infirmary days, Rose and Joe made certain that Jack always had a hefty supply of books to ponder. They did not tire of reminding Jack of the graces he was receiving by offering his pain and disappointments in union with

Jesus, the suffering servant Redeemer. They always assured Jack that his sickness was a spiritual gift with eternal value. Kathleen seemed to understand Jack's spiritual path as no one else until Jacqueline Bouvier entered JFK's life.

After the convivial voyage on the *Isle de France*, Kathleen became so homesick at her remote, austere convent school that Rose could not bear her daughter's pain. The sensitive mother quickly arranged for Kathleen to transfer to a less austere, more sophisticated Sacred Heart Convent boarding school in the Parisian suburb of Neuilly where she would be closer to Jack. Rose and Joe both hoped that Jack and Kathleen would meet on weekends and holidays to share the youthful delights of London and Paris. Joe was quite pleased with his choice of education for Jack as he believed it important for his sons to understand the political thinking prevalent in their times. Jack, however, showed no interest in the eminent professor's views on fascism, communism, Nazism, or even President Roosevelt's New Deal. It was a time of celebration for young JFK, who had quietly decided with his sister Kathleen during their transatlantic crossing to develop his social life by dating fascinating young ladies.

As he began this social pursuit in London, however, the mysterious hand of fate interrupted. Jack became so ill with jaundice that Joe Senior was forced to arrange for his immediate return to the United States for medical treatment. As sickly Jack was forced to return home, but not wanting medical issues to cast him adrift while his peers were happily ensconced in their university lives, he arranged to matriculate at Princeton University in New Jersey where his Prep School friend Lem Billings was studying.⁶⁵ By December, the hand of fate scorched him again and Jack was necessarily hospitalized in Boston for his many severe, as yet undiagnosable, illnesses. Enduring even more grueling tests that would yield no remedies for his infirmities, JFK had the consolation of cheerful visits from his maternal grandfather, still known affectionately in Boston as Mayor Honey Fitz, who loved to regale his namesake with heroic stories about his world travels on behalf of historic Boston. The retired Boston mayor filled ailing Jack's imagination with political tales that were laced with his delightful humor and endearing affection. Jack, however, was getting no better, and finding no specific cures for his ailments, he was discharged with instructions to rest. JFK, still quite ill, returned to his family winter home in Palm Beach, Florida. After two months of convalescence, his health showed no improvement. Jack's worried father and mother sent him to a health spa-ranch in Arizona with firm instructions to recover his health.

While far away from family and friends in Arizona, and having no immediate family in New Jersey, but rightfully concerned about his illusive health, Jack decided to forgo Princeton. He enrolled at Harvard, his father's *alma mater*, where his older brother Joe had established himself as a scholar and athlete. At JFK's lanky six feet stature, but barely weighing 150 pounds, he managed to play on Harvard's junior varsity football and golf teams, and the varsity swim team. He also found time to serve on the business board of the *Harvard Crimson* newspaper. When JFK finally selected his university major, few were surprised that he chose government, which Harvard's eminent faculty laced heavily with history and economics.

IDEALS

Maturing JFK, kindly, intelligent, and charming by nature, was popular with his Harvard peers. By the summer of 1937, Jack travelled again to Europe, this time with Lem Billings, his lifelong friend from Choate. Filled with historical stories of brave men and wars and opportunities for valor and greatness, they enjoyed visiting major cities with their fortified castles, remnants of forts and actual battlefields with monuments reflecting triumphant battles on the European continent. Of course, having heard of miraculous physical healings at the famous religious shrine of Our Lady of Lourdes in France, Jack and his Episcopalian pal Lem were curious enough to investigate and possibly experience the prolific miracles they had heard about the celebrated shrine at Lourdes. Lem's dad was a noted physician in Pittsburgh and had found famous medical miracles at Lourdes to be fascinating. Since both Jack and Lem were spiritually disciplined within their faith traditions to possess immense respect for, and awe of the Blessed Virgin Mary, the devout young men who never missed Sunday services prayed fervently in Lourdes's great Basilica of Our Lady built in 1876. They investigated the exact place in the Grotto of Massabielle where Mary, the Holy Mother of Jesus, was seen by fourteen-year-old Saint Bernadette between February 11 and July 16, 1858. Jack and Lem also visited the poverty-stricken saint's domicile and bathed in Lourdes's mysterious healing waters.[66] There is no known written record of the religious experience either young seeker may have experienced at the extraordinary Marian Shrine of Lourdes where miracles continue to this day.

As the young Ivy Leaguers continued their European journey, JFK was eagerly receptive to the opinions of his educated

European peers. He heard disturbing nuances envisaging world war within unsubstantiated political attitudes of contemporary elites, especially in Germany where Nazism was brewing. The two American college students encountered extreme German arrogance and hostility not only toward them, but against the very fabric of American liberty so dear to the heart of young Bostonian John F. Kennedy, whose imagination still thrilled with revolutionary war images of places he had visited with his siblings during early childhood outings with their patriotic mother.

Jack could never forget New Englander Henry Wadsworth Longfellow's inspiring patriotic poem, "Paul Revere's Ride," which he recited word for word to Lem as a way of expressing his disdain for the arrogance of young European elites who failed to comprehend the personal cost of American freedom.[67] Not to be outdone, Lem recounted thrilling tales of great American frontiersman soldiers, including George Washington himself, whose heroism tamed the wilderness west of the Allegheny Mountains, including Lem's hometown of Pittsburgh. Jack, of course, shared Lem's admiration for Daniel Boone and physically powerful Davy Crockett, who purportedly triumphed in hand-to-hand combat with mountain bears on the American frontier.[68]

The following summer of 1938 found JFK working in the US embassy in London where his father, Joe Senior, served as US Ambassador to the Court of Saint James. Jack's parents and his younger sisters, especially Kathleen, noticed that Jack seemed to enjoy his popularity in London social circles as the American ambassador's privileged, bachelor son. Rose and Joe were seemingly unaware that JFK was quick to perceive tensions among rivaling European powers that were openly discussed at London's brilliant tea parties, dances, horse races, and even at simple social gatherings at local pubs. Concerned that Europe was on the brink of a World War, Jack thoughtfully returned in the autumn of 1938 to complete his university studies at Harvard.

Excelling in his government courses, JFK was able to spend his spring semester of 1939 in London at the US embassy. He was certainly aware of his ambassador father's unpopular, outspoken isolationist views. Jack suspected his dad's pragmatic isolationism was sourced in Joe Senior's lifelong aversion to war, coupled with his respect for Germany's advanced manufacturing and economic prowess that no other nation on the European Continent matched. JFK tried unsuccessfully to convince his dad of dangers to the US homeland inherent in the outspoken attitudes of young German elites. Joe Senior, however, had his own firmly rooted international business opinions about the extreme folly of war. He was familiar with the lack of military preparedness within the US and lobbied Washington continuously for neutrality in the event of European conflict. The American ambassador sincerely hoped and prayed that US neutrality would protect his country from participation in yet another world war.

Busy Joe Senior remained seemingly uninterested in his second son's intellectual assessments of impending World War that would inevitably suck the United States into its quicksand. Joe Senior's clear, concise, outspoken goal was to keep the US out of war at all costs.[69] Astute JFK, however, knew it was already too late for that noble goal to be fact. Returning to Harvard for his senior year, Jack wrote his 148-page senior honor's thesis entitled *"Appeasement at Munich: The Inevitable Result of the*

Slowness of Conversion of the British Democracy to Change from a Disarmament Policy to Rearmament Policy."

The work itself intrigued US publishing powerbrokers who saw its long-term value as a book for diplomatic policymakers worldwide. Joe Senior's longtime friend Henry R. Luce, esteemed publisher of popular magazines such as *Time, Life, Fortune,* and *Sports Illustrated,* was delighted to write the foreword of Jack's book. Arthur Krock, another friend of Joe Senior, who was former bureau chief of the *New York Times,* was so convinced of the value of JFK's work that he gladly handled the editing of Jack's senior thesis. The result was John F. Kennedy's best-selling book published in 1940 entitled *Why England Slept.* Admittedly, the title was a takeoff of Winston Churchill's highly popular book *While England Slept.*

JFK undertook a strenuous book tour throughout the entire US during the summer of 1940. Crowds found young Jack to be witty, intelligent and caring. His controversial book was well received throughout the country, but JFK encountered and understood outspoken opposition to the US becoming involved militarily in Europe's horrible "war squabbles." Memories of World War I led many Americans to believe that Europe was actually incapable of managing its own conflicts. Many civilians who spoke with JFK at his book signings told him disdainfully that they were unwilling to ever again let Washington bureaucrats shed American blood for Europeans who could never understand the inherent spirit of liberty that protected the American way of life.

In September of 1940, to the horror of many war-adverse Americans, the US Congress passed the first peacetime

IDEALS

conscription in US history, the Selective Training and Service Act, which required all men between the ages of twenty-one and thirty-five to register with local draft boards. Deferral from military service was granted to students enrolled in academic institutions of higher learning. Always conscious of his fragile health, and exhausted after his strenuous book tour, Jack Kennedy decided to enroll in the Graduate School of Business at Stanford University for the fall semester in Palo Alto, California where he would study international business. He had not yet learned that there are no perfect climates on earth, even though some are better than others. He had yet to learn that world peace is a divine gift that must be earned.[70] JFK remained deeply concerned about looming World War II. He recognized that European and Asian conflicts would inevitably draw the US into combat simply to ensure the very survival of his nation and its way of life founded in liberty and justice for all. Upon completion of his one semester graduate courses at Stanford, Jack was deemed 4-F by his local draft board which meant to eager young JFK that he was medically unfit for service on behalf of his beloved country.

Giving himself time to ponder his next step, Jack joined his mother and younger sister Eunice on their journey through eight Latin American countries. He listened and astutely questioned local leaders, clergymen, and elites who graciously entertained his devout Catholic mother while Eunice and he tagged along. He also prayed the rosary with his mom and sister and worshipped with them at morning Mass in some of the most beautiful churches in Latin America built by sacrifices of faith-filled missionaries and European immigrants. Rose and

Eunice were delighted to have this special time with Jack, who was often referred to as the sickly, second son of the former US Ambassador to the Court of Saint James by elites who welcomed them. JFK's charm, wit, confidence, and heightened intelligence, however, reassured his mother and sister that the best was yet to come for Jack. His failing health was another matter, and Rose knew that world war spares no one

In late fall of 1941, Joe Senior, with deep reservations, but responding to Jack's constant prodding, prevailed upon a former London US Naval colleague to obtain another medical exam for JFK which his son passed. Jack's former 4-F health record now listed simple "usual childhood diseases." JFK was commissioned a navy ensign in the US Naval Reserve in October of 1941 and was assigned to the Office of Naval Intelligence in the Washington, DC bureau. In a surprise attack on December 7, 1941, the empire of Japan bombed the American naval fleet and airfields at Pearl Harbor in Hawaii killing nearly 2,500 civilians and US personnel. Nineteen navy ships were destroyed or severely damaged. Fortuitously, three aircraft carriers of the US Pacific fleet were out at sea at the time. The next day, December 8, 1941, US President Franklin D. Roosevelt identified the Pearl Harbor attack as "a day that will live in infamy." With only one dissenting vote, the US Congress declared war on Japan. Three days later, on December 11, 1941, Japan's allies Germany and Italy declared war on the United States. As the war intensified, Jack became thoroughly bored manning a bureaucratic desk in Washington, DC where he felt useless and requested a transfer to midshipman's school at Northwestern University in Chicago, Illinois. By January of 1942, he was promoted to

IDEALS

Lieutenant Junior Grade and assigned to the Sixth Naval District in Charleston, South Carolina.

Shipmates saw JFK sleep on an improvised plywood board, which he told them when directly asked that he hoped it would ameliorate his back issues. Jack quietly realized he had severe back deformities that were extremely painful. In 1943, after sixty days of combat training, Jack Kennedy was given command of his own wooden hull motor patrol torpedo boat believed to be a fast and highly maneuverable combat weapon that was used extensively in the South Pacific war theater. Jack's next billet was the site of the famous Rendova Island Invasion (from June 30 to July 2, 1943), which was the South Pacific base for PT boats.[71] While serving seventeen months on active duty in the South Pacific, JFK had many opportunities to exhibit his moral strength and heroic regard for fellow sailors under his command.

None could match the dark night of August 1, 1943, when John F. Kennedy's *PT-109* was split in half on impact by an unseen Japanese destroyer that was later identified as the *Amagiri*. Two of JFK's crewmen were instantly killed when the *Amagiri* struck the *PT-109* forward of the starboard forward torpedo tube, ripping away the entire starboard aft side of the boat. The destroyer's wake had dispersed *PT-109*'s fuel every which way. Aware that the remnants of his boat could burst into flames at any moment, Kennedy ordered crew who still clung to what was left of the crippled *PT-109* to abandon ship immediately. After fuel fires subsided, JFK constantly reassured his disheartened surviving crew. He personally assisted weaker swimmers to cling for nine grueling hours to a type of long log which was all that remained of their PT boat. The distraught *PT-109* crew could only hope and pray all the while for a rescue team to appear.

As their boat remnant sank, Skipper Kennedy, fortuitously a strong, unafraid swimmer heroically undertook to bring his crew to safety on a nearby Island. Although that five-hour ordeal, swimming in turbulent mine, barracuda, and shark infested waters with his highly traumatized crew toward an unknown, possibly enemy-occupied island in the Pacific Ocean, would haunt Kennedy for the rest of his life, he could never forget his two crew members who died on impact during his watch. After a harrowing week during which Kennedy demonstrated heroic and exemplary leadership on behalf of his men, the surviving crew of *PT-109* was rescued by an allied New Zealand army team at 5:30 a.m. on August 8.[72]

During the entire time that Jack was missing in action, although Joe Senior had chosen not to tell Rose that Jack was MIA, his mom experienced horrible nightmares about him suffering alone and far away from help. Most prayerful mothers and even some of their more prayerful offspring understand this inexplicable, lifelong soul intimacy between mother and child. Although her husband, wishing to spare her, had not let her know that Jack was officially MIA, Rose discerned that her Jack was in trouble, and she greatly increased her prayers and sacrifices, storming heaven constantly for her second-born son during the entire time that he was missing in action and presumed dead. There is no known record of Joe Senior's experience during his second son's horrific difficulties in the South Pacific war zone. No one seems to know how Jack's older brother Joe endured his beloved younger brother's Solomon Island saga.

IDEALS

No record survives of Kathleen's experience during Jack's *PT-109* difficulties. Hard facts demonstrate that the mysterious hand of fate would save JFK but very soon reach down and take both Joe Jr. and Kathleen in the blink of an eye. No one knows why.

One can only imagine the joy both Rose and Joe experienced when news arrived that their second son was rescued. Jack's back pains unsurprisingly escalated after his naval service in the Solomon Islands. He silently endured what was then medically diagnosed as severe colitis resulting from battle trauma. After ten days of medical rest, Jack Kennedy returned to combat duty in the South Pacific. Now, he wore a stronger brace on his back and was highly concerned that fellow soldiers on active duty were suffering the physical effects of the war in many ways seen and unseen. By November, enduring unbearable stomach issues and excruciating lower back pain, JFK took a thirty-day medical leave and returned to the US. After more agonizing medical tests at Mayo Clinic in Rochester, MN, immediate back surgery was recommended. Missing his family and still worried about his traumatized crew members, JFK chose to forego back surgery at that time and returned to Palm Beach. When his relentless back pain escalated, Rose and Joe Senior insisted that Jack obtain a second medical opinion. Consequently, suffering JFK went to the New England Baptist Hospital in Boston for more tests. Again, corrective back surgery was prescribed.

Having served in combat in the Pacific for nearly two years, Jack Kennedy was deeply sensitive to the often-soundless suffering other troops patiently endured in the war zones. Anyone who could breathe seemed to be sent into battle. JFK, however, realized there was a global war to be won. He returned to active duty, but this time he was assigned to a PT base in Miami where he lent his hands-on experience to US Navy engineers working on upgrading PT boat design. Stateside in Miami, during a required routine medical checkup, it was surprisingly discovered that JFK was suffering from severe malaria. He was sent to Chelsea Naval Hospital near Boston for treatment. There, routine x-rays revealed that Jack also had a ruptured disc in his lower back. By early 1944, his untreated spastic colitis was now diagnosed as diffuse duodenitis with complications from severe spastic colitis at nearby Lahey Clinic in Boston.

On August 12, 1944, JFK's beloved, greatly admired older brother Joe Jr., a highly skilled Navy pilot, had volunteered to fly the US Navy's PB4Y-1 Liberator bomber loaded with 22,000 pounds of explosives on a highly classified top-secret combat mission. The plane unexpectedly exploded and Lieutenant Joseph P. Kennedy, Jr. was killed in action. The Kennedy family was devastated. It was some consolation that their lost firstborn son was posthumously awarded the Navy Cross for valor. All Joe Senior's nightmares were becoming reality. His natural personal discipline and intolerance for weak humans unable to solve problems tortured him as he struggled alone with the Lord trying to assimilate his horrific grief. Rose, the sorrowful mother, increased her prayer life but spoke little.

Very sick JFK had undergone back surgery at New England Baptist Hospital on June 23, 1944, after diagnosis at Chelsea Naval Hospital. But Jack was slow to recover even though he had convalesced at a navy center in the warm, dry, healing climate of Phoenix, Arizona. Unfortunately, his intestinal disorders intensified; this infirmity created nearly unbearable stomach pain coupled with severe, unrelenting back pain. Physical weakness laced with misery became the lot of the young navy officer. Stoic JFK, remembering his deeply admired older brother Joe, discretely shared his unrelenting suffering with no one. He knew he was simply one of many US military personnel who endured war's hidden aches and pains.

THREE

Politics that Prevent War

Double, double toil and trouble.
Fire burn and cauldron bubble . . .
for a charm of powerful trouble,
like a hell-broth boil and bubble.[73]
—William Shakespeare

Jack Kennedy continued to hear the call of duty; his aspirations to protect his country had deepened after Joe's death. Honorable people of all times understand his patriotism. Though he was painfully aware of the brutal cost of liberty, he believed defensive war is a duty that no decent person avoids. When friends and colleagues tried to dissuade him from returning to the war zone, patriot JFK countered with his gratitude for his American heritage. He was adamant that his difficulties were minor in comparison to the great heroes, past, present, and future who had or would water American buds of liberty with their own blood. Joe Jr. was never far from Jack's prayers and penances patiently endured for purposes far higher than himself. His faith assured him that life is eternal, and death is but a passage to a higher life form.[74]

Difficult as it was for Rose and Joe suffering grief only Gold Star parents understand, they comforted one another in their immeasurable sorrows, reminding each other of their shared responsibility as Christians to make their limited time on earth count for the common good.[75] Privately, Rose and Joe laced their unconsolable sorrow at the loss of their first-born in faith-filled prayer that Joe Jr.'s life sacrifice for his country would be rewarded both in their beloved United States and in the Eternal Kingdom.[76]

War-scarred JFK well understood Joe Jr.'s life sacrifice for his country. Believing that people constantly face off against invisible principalities and powers intent on destroying all vestiges of peaceful civility in families, cities and countries, Jack knew neither he nor his brother Joe would ever willingly give in to darkness.[77] His ancient Catholic Christian faith reminded him that unseen, thoroughly malevolent beings easily stir up the unaware, inducing them to wage war against themselves and others; in effect, abrogating human decency.[78] Like his valiant war-hero brother Joe Jr., Jack would have none of it.[79]

Prayerful JFK had recognized an invisible hand of fate guiding him in the South Pacific. Though he was heartbroken about his beloved older brother Joe's horrible death in the line of duty, he knew much about reliance upon Kind Providence inherent in the writings of the founders of the American Republic. He was also knowledgeable about the spiritual feats of the pilgrims who first landed on the shores of the American continent with nothing to guide them but their faith, trust, and obedience to the calls of Divine Providence. Patriotic Jack Kennedy also recognized that there is a time to be born and a time to die, which no man or power under the sun can dispute or change.[80]

Like his childhood folk hero Paul Revere, duty-bound JFK determined to do his best as he bravely ventured into the dark night of the unknown on the frontier of American liberty. Even though severely compromised health would continue to plague twenty-eight-year-old Jack Kennedy for the rest of his life, the end of World War II drew nearer. Lieutenant John F. Kennedy was honorably discharged from the navy in late winter of 1945. Jack received the Navy and Marine Corp medal for heroic service. He was also awarded the Purple Heart for his war injuries. Like too many heroic, silent war veterans, JFK would never recover his health.

Intensely interested in the politics of world affairs, and firmly believing in the possibility of grace-filled, peaceful dispute resolution, Jack decided to use whatever time he had left on earth, painful as it might be, to create a more peaceful, comfortable life not only for himself, but also for others throughout the world who would be willing to exert effort and the discipline necessary for freedom and prosperity. Having observed his dad's tireless work to provide generously for his family, JFK was aware that debt bondage, limited resources, back-breaking labor, ethnic, racial, and gender discrimination were worldwide impediments to liberty's inherent luxury. He was also aware that as mysterious as it might seem at any given time, all things work together for good for those who love God and remain faithful in good times and difficult times too.[81] He was quietly proud of his older brother's faithfulness, even in facing death.[82]

Jack Kennedy, the *magna cum laude* Harvard graduate would always be a Boston boy at heart who believed that American heroes of yesteryear who sacrificed their lives, their fortunes, and their sacred honor to establish the United States of America as the freest country in the world had created a blueprint for every nation seeking liberty, peace, and prosperity for its citizens. JFK may or may not have known then that he, like his cherished older brother Joe (and his younger brother Bobby) would one day choose to lay down his own life on the cornerstone of American liberty.

With his family wealth and connections, Jack was able to undertake a job with Hearst Newspapers as a roving world reporter. He wrote an article entitled "Let's Try an Experiment in Peace" in which he cautioned against an arms race, which he believed would only lead to more hostilities. He worried about those in charge of weapons of mass destruction who are constantly tempted to use them, and especially those who would engage without sufficient knowledge of their perceived enemy's intentions. Many heard Jack muse that nefarious as they are, destructive weapons do not, nor can they, bring peace. The South Pacific war hero was aware that weapons of mass destruction are indeed cruel weapons of death that create more problems than they solve.

JFK seriously studied the significant political, geographical and economic reconstruction of post-World War II Europe. In late summer of 1945, Harry Truman was now US President and Europe was being carved up by victorious allies Winston Churchill, Josef Stalin, and Harry Truman at the Potsdam Conference in Germany. Although John F. Kennedy grew up in the halls of power and wealth, he always resisted snobbery. Some have pondered whether health problems kept him free of the machismo evident in Truman, Churchill, and Stalin as they divided the spoils of World War II at Potsdam. Having traveled throughout Europe, including Russia and Eastern Europe before the Second World War, and always a resolute student of history, JFK feared that hardliner Soviet policymakers carried hidden wounds of anger and pierced pride as they unconsciously emulated the entitled, now despised Russian aristocracy.

Although enduring poor health and constant pain, JFK was on a journalistic assignment in London in autumn of 1945 when he was diagnosed with a severe flare-up of Addison's disease, a rare autoimmune disorder that attacks human bones. It was little consolation that his younger sister Eunice was also afflicted with Addison's disease, which is a lifelong, atypical endocrine disorder. At that time, sickly Jack Kennedy was told by knowledgeable medical experts in London that his health was so compromised that he dared not expect to live beyond the age of forty-five.

Both Russia and China were poor countries in 1945. Their vast, mostly uneducated populations knew little or nothing of the ideals of personal responsibility and commensurate personal freedom flowing from liberty's requirement of self-regulating moral behavior. Many wise policymakers whom Jack Kennedy admired spoke openly that Communist ideology would drag the freedom-loving US into a Third World War from which it could not recover.[83]

Jack Kennedy believed that the American way of life was superior to any other system, simply because all people everywhere want and need liberty. Astute World War II veterans were aware that Lenin's insurgent tactics place a high value on deception as revolution spreads like a virus that enslaves the unwary.[84] Jack Kennedy was quick to recognize the ongoing threat to his homeland of nuclear weapons of mass destruction, especially those of the trigger-happy, nuclear armed Soviets, suffused as the entire Russian nation was, in atheistic, totalitarian Communism. Those who place no value on any human life but their own are quick to kill. Chinese revolutionary Chairman Mao, also known as Mao Zedong, had Communist China on the march against US backed General Chiang Kai-shek, leader of the Republic of China. JFK quickly recognized the futility of their political goals. More significantly, he saw the human cost of their warlike ways.

As young Jack Kennedy was returning home on board the Queen Mary from his fact-finding mission in England in 1945, he became so gravely ill that he was given the Sacramental Last Rites of the Catholic Church.[85] Kennedy survived but required nearly a year to recover some modicum of stamina before again undertaking his duties. No one is known to have questioned JFK about the spiritual component of his near-death experience. Many combat veterans are permanently but silently scarred by battle, some worse than others. As JFK weighed his options, he had many material advantages that were coupled with his intense desire to influence global decisionmakers who hold the levers of peace or war. Lurking in the back of Jack's mind was the loving influence of his maternal grandfather Honey Fitz who had filled his Kennedy grandchildren with exhilarating political stories about his joys and triumphs as mayor of Boston. After thoughtfully weighing his options, JFK decided to run for an open seat in the Eleventh Congressional District of Massachusetts. Colleagues who would help Kennedy on his congressional campaign recognized that the candidate was capable of intense personal sacrifice for reasons Kennedy never discussed.

Fundamentally, after his harrowing experiences in the Solomon Islands, and realizing the effects of Addison's disease on his body, Jack Kennedy was somewhat introverted. He enjoyed being alone to intellectually devour stimulating books while he processed his personal losses as he reached for equanimity. In deep prayer, JFK found consolation and renewed courage. Rallies and intermingling with voters were physical challenges that would be difficult for him not only because of his poor health and many physical limitations but also his natural desire for privacy. As much as he respected volunteers and their commitments to serve, JFK learned from them that his group skills and public speaking ability were seriously undeveloped as he began his run for Congress. With their guidance, he studied and honed his skills to become a formidable opponent. Jack Kennedy's loyal family rallied around their sickly, surviving second son and surrounded him with enthusiasm and hands-on help.

Always comfortable with blue-collar, working-class constituents, mainly of Irish or Italian descent, JFK happily listened to their political goals hour after hour and encouraged their aspirations. He deeply appreciated that these were his people, and he found immense satisfaction in serving them. Some observed that the spiritual side of John F. Kennedy was profoundly touched as he personally overcame his own physical difficulties to walk among the adult children of immigrant families that had given up their own pathetically compromised homelands and families far away seeking a fairer way of life for themselves and their children. Early Massachusetts immigrants and their offspring had offered their backs and hands and hopes to carry out the ideals and aspirations of the founders of the USA, and John F. Kennedy sincerely believed his war-scarred generation should do no less. He felt immensely privileged to serve his beloved constituents. Love covers a multitude of human differences.

Increased Social Security benefits and affordable housing for homecoming troops were foremost needs among the voters who swamped young war hero JFK's rallies. Severe antipathy for war was evident in the sorrowful faces of those who had lost loved ones as had Jack Kennedy during the European and Pacific conflicts. Consequently, JFK reassured anyone who would listen to him that American peace required superior armaments primarily as a deterrent to bully nations seeking to steal what others had achieved through hard work and sacrifice. His constituents seemed to resonate with his logic. Kennedy money was useful for obtaining the services of public relations firms and newspaper support during JFK's campaign. Jack was adamant in calling for indifferent people to actually discipline themselves to cast their votes. He often mentioned the bloody sacrifices of his fallen crew members in the Pacific as a stimulant for apathetic nonvoters. JFK was eloquent in defending American ideals as he identified himself a stalwart champion of the working class in the Eleventh Congressional District of Massachusetts. His respect for hard-working Americans knew no bounds.[86]

There was a national need for coherence among all American citizens who were deeply fragmented by the long, grueling war effort. Jack faced head-on the social problems and post–World War II hardships that now fueled dissonance among diverse populations, not only throughout the country, but globally. Left unchecked, such conflict could cripple effective government, and JFK intended to do something—anything and everything—to bring healing, comfort and inspiration to war ravaged families everywhere. Obviously, his constituents recognized JFK's capacity for heroic sacrifice on their behalf. Twenty-nine-year-old John F. Kennedy won 72 percent of the vote in his congressional district. Rose and Joe, and especially his grandfather, Honey Fitz, were overjoyed. Many political observers mentioned the political effectiveness of tea parties hosted by JFK's mom and sisters that entertained lady voters who greatly appreciated experiencing such refinement. During those late afternoon tea parties for voters in the Eleventh Congressional District of Massachusetts, tables were splendidly covered in sparkling white linen and laden with delicacies to delight every taste bud. Thousands of ladies wearing hats, gloves, and their best Sunday dresses heard the young war hero candidate discuss his plans to make life better for each of them and their families. The pleasures of refinement—a comfortable home, enough food, clothes, and medical care, recreation and good education—Kennedy believed, were the aspirations of every hard-working American who longed for peace.

On January 3, 1947, Congressman John F. Kennedy had a voice, humble as it was, that he planned to use to increase the well-being not only of all his loyal constituents, but also of anyone who would listen to him. Friends and campaign workers later said that Jack Kennedy, even as a young congressman, would do his utmost so that all people of good conscience could benefit. As for sickly, pain-ridden JFK, he suspected that a mysterious hand of fate had finally enabled him to rise above his own weaknesses laced with constant pain for the benefit of many far needier than he.

During the congressional summer recess of 1947, Jack travelled to Europe. His first stop was a month-long visit with his recent war-widowed sister Kathleen at her in-law's Lismore Castle in County Wexford, Ireland. Kathleen was overjoyed to have her brother all to herself for a while. She invited well-connected political friends to visit hoping to make Jack's holiday special. What she seemed not to know was that Jack was deeply interested in his family roots. He knew that he had ancestors in the little Irish town of New Ross, about fifty miles east of Lismore Castle. He borrowed a car from Kathleen and invited her friend Pamela Churchill to accompany him while his sister played a round of golf. They found a little white house on the edge of the village of New Ross with a thatched roof, no indoor plumbing and chickens and geese filling the tiny yard. JFK was delighted that he found his third cousins, a stalwart man and his wife and their many children that day. Of course, the US Congressman asked what he could do for his distant relatives. They demurred but finally admitted that a ride in Kennedy's borrowed station wagon would be marvelous. Kennedy later would occasionally mention that this family visit was the highlight of his European fact-finding mission. Kathleen, however, was unamused by her brother's ancestorial exuberance.[87]

A year later, in 1948, JFK's beloved sister Katheen Kennedy Cavendish, Marchioness of Hartington, was suddenly killed in an airplane crash in France. Kathleen's death was a hard blow to Jack who wept at her passing.[88] He had comforted her when her

British husband was killed in action in Belgium five weeks after their wedding in May of 1944. He and Kathleen, both mourning their brother, Joe Jr.'s, recent death, had sought relief from their suffering at Hyannis Port. Jack, still on active duty then, was recovering from failed back surgery at the New England Baptist Hospital in Boston. Their pain was so intense that they decided to have a word or two with Jesus in the Blessed Sacrament who was quite used to hearing their complaints as they looked for divine solace at the nearby church of their childhood, St. Francis Xavier.[89] Kneeling together before the golden tabernacle on the high altar, they realized they had no choice but to surrender to the mysterious hand of fate that guides all things, including the foolishness and mistakes of unconscious leaders.[90] They realized theirs was not to reason why but simply to do and die.[91] Their faith increased that day: in spite of their own difficulties, they both trusted that their "higher power" Jesus, inexplicably present in the Blessed Sacrament,[92] would most certainly bring some good out of their pain and sorrow.

JFK's hero Winston Churchill had immense concern about the global treachery of Communist Russia. Few other leaders at the time shared his concerns. Churchill claimed he observed a Soviet iron curtain looming over the entire European continent. Although he spiritually was viewed at best as an agnostic, if not an atheist,[93] Winston Churchill was aware of the Marian prophecies flowing from Fatima. His influence upon Harry Truman may have induced the US President to lobby for approval of the Marshall Plan to rebuild the bombed-out towns and villages of Europe. Truman also supported the formation of NATO, the North Atlantic Treaty Organization, a military alliance for mutual defense among the Western nations. Congressman Kennedy, who believed the US should do more to protect itself against the rising Communist threat coming out of the Soviet Union, was in favor of both the Marshall Plan and NATO.

JFK may have believed that Harry Truman and his diplomats frittered away what young US soldiers had earned with their blood. Consequently, Congressman Jack Kennedy was eager to have his voice matter even more in the Senate chambers. Evolving geopolitical currents had made it clear that the times were calling Jack Kennedy to strategize his political move to the halls of the US Senate. In 1949, the Soviet Union detonated its first nuclear weapon. JFK had Washington friends who worked at the Atomic Energy Commission (the AOC) who discreetly informed him of the scientific dangers of nuclear weapons of mass destruction to humankind and the planet Earth. By 1950, the Korean War shocked the largely unprepared Western nations. Kennedy joined his voice with California's young Republican Congressman Richard Nixon, who espoused anti-communist rhetoric at every opportunity.

Always choosing to make his own decisions, sickly Congressman JFK travelled to Europe again in early 1951. His goal was to assess the present danger of Soviet Russia and Communist China as US troops, along with those of other Western nations, ploughed their way through the bloody Korean War. Again, in autumn of 1951, Jack Kennedy travelled abroad. This time he visited Israel, Iran, India, Pakistan, French Indochina, Singapore, Thailand, Japan, and Korea. JFK astutely recognized that as American democratic influence in those regions weakened, rightful nationalist aspirations of locals escalated. Kennedy was concerned that the largely uneducated masses in these developing areas would be easy prey for Soviet Marxist revolutionary deceptions that would mercilessly enslave them and their future generations. Communist ideology places no value on individuals.[94] Unfortunately, Marxist Communism spreads like a silent infection that greedily consumes people, slowly digests their minds, then mercilessly spits them out as mere cogs in a vast machine that government overlords control for their own benefit. Marxist Communism effectively exterminates the personal freedom of entire populations. JFK conjectured that as captive populations grow in education and moral self-awareness, Marxist Communism becomes so personally restricting that enlightened people simply cast it off as they strive for liberty in thought, word, and deed.

By 1952, the war-weary US elected Republican General Dwight D. Eisenhower as President by a wide margin. John F. Kennedy narrowly defeated Boston Brahmin Senator Henry Cabot Lodge by approximately 70,000 votes. Massachusetts minorities had flocked to the Irish Catholic war hero with high hopes that, finally, their voices would be heard in high places. And so, they were. Eisenhower had promised to swiftly end the Korean War, and he did so quickly. Marxist Communism, however, continued to infiltrate the US, especially through naïve elites unaware of its malevolent tentacles. No one could foresee the bipolar balance of terror that would divide the world into Western democratic nations and the Soviet Marxist Communist Eastern Bloc determined to wipe out the populations of the earth with first strike nuclear weapons of mass destruction, perhaps even on a hardliner leader's misinformed action.[95]

Senator John F. Kennedy disagreed with President Eisenhower on some of his US-Soviet foreign policy issues. Eisenhower wanted high-powered strategic nuclear weapons as a deterrent to Eastern Bloc malfeasance. No one seemed to know if Eisenhower was knowledgeable about the global danger to the environment that nuclear weapons produce. Jack Kennedy actually detested the global "Massive Retaliation Strategy" because he was intellectually aware of the danger of human miscalculation with military assets that could inadvertently trigger worldwide annihilation through a nuclear holocaust.[96]

As for his own personal life direction, JFK retained devotion to his Church and the solace he found worshipping alone at Mass. Historian Arthur Schlesinger, Jr., who worked closely with Kennedy, would observe only what he personally knew when he wrote: "Kennedy's religion was humane rather than doctrinal. He was a Catholic as Franklin Roosevelt was an Episcopalian—because he was born into it, lived in it, and expected to die in it . . . He felt an immense sense of fellowship with Pope John XXIII . . . his basic attitude was wholly compatible with the sophisticated theology of Jesuits like Father John Courtney Murray[97]—whom he greatly admired . . . Above all, he showed that there was no conflict between Catholicism and modernity, no bar to full Catholic participation in American society . . . In fact, he was intensely committed to a vision of America and the world, and committed with equal intensity to the use of reason and power to achieve that vision . . . He was fascinated by the Founding Fathers—how a small and underdeveloped nation could have produced men of such genius."[98] At the signing of the Constitution of the United States in 1787, the population of the new nation was approximately only 1 percent of the population of the world. By 1952, the US population comprised only 5.8 percent of the world's population. Contemporary historians would not recognize the deep Christian faith enveloping John F. Kennedy's ethos from earliest childhood through four near-death experiences simply because that was Kennedy's choice. He would always remember his dad's warning: "Never wear your faith publicly." JFK did not.

Kennedy often asked of the intellectual community: "Where are the scholar-statesmen?" He liked to invite others to a position he personally adapted as his own: "Keep strong, if possible. In any case, keep cool. Have unlimited patience. Never corner an opponent and always assist him to save his face. Put yourself in his shoes—so as to see things through his eyes. Avoid self-righteousness like the devil—nothing is so self-blinding."[99] Like many great leaders, Kennedy saw history "in its massive movements as shaped by forces beyond man's control."[100] Some call this Divine Providence. Others simply acknowledge the mystery of fate's invisible, guiding hand.

* * *

September 12, 1953, was a perfect autumn day. Senator John F. Kennedy married the former society debutante of the year, beautiful Jacqueline Lee Bouvier. As many as 700 invited guests witnessed the Catholic bride and groom exchange vows at Saint Mary's Church in Newport, Rhode Island. After the nuptial High Mass, a lavish reception for 1,200 guests followed at the estate of the bride's stepfather, Standard Oil heir Hugh

Dudley Auchincloss, Jr. The Holy Sacrament of Matrimony unites a Christian man and woman in lawful marriage. The Savior Himself raised the contract of marriage to a supernatural Sacrament whose outward sign is the mutual consent of the bride and groom expressed by words or signs in accordance with the laws of the Church. The whole essence of the marriage contract raised to the level of Holy Sacramental Matrimony consists in husband and wife declaring by word or sign that they freely surrender their lives to each other for life to aid one another in securing the salvation of their souls; to propagate the human race by bringing children into the world to serve God; to prevent sins against the sacred virtue of purity by faithfully obeying the spiritual laws of the marriage state.[101]

It was obvious to most guests that Jacqueline and Jack Kennedy were deeply in love with each other. They were kindred spirits in many ways. Both were vociferous readers who enjoyed travel and the exchange of ideas. Although neither bride nor groom had ideal health, they were stalwart athletes who knew their physical limitations. They shared the same intellectual Catholic religion, were educated in elite secular schools and both had experienced the advantages of privileged upbringings. The couple had met at a dinner party in Georgetown hosted by JFK's good friend Charles Bartlett, the nationally syndicated Washington correspondent for the *Chattanooga Times*. Jack Kennedy's and Jacqueline Bouvier's immediate attraction to one another was obvious to the other guests. At that time, twenty-four-year-old Jackie was the inquiring photographer at the Washington, DC newspaper where Jack's beloved, now deceased sister, Kathleen, had worked before the war. JFK, a thirty-six-year-old bachelor senator had never before encountered a woman with Jacqueline Bouvier's depth, beauty, intellectual strength, and charm.

In spring of 1953, Jack gave his bride-to-be a two-carat diamond and emerald engagement ring and they immediately began making plans for their autumn nuptials.[102] Of course, both families were delighted. Rose and Joe were particularly pleased with beautiful Jacqueline Bouvier, whom they believed was a perfect wife for their second son. It was important to them that Jacqueline become aware of Jack's many infirmities so that her consent to Holy Sacramental Matrimony would be grounded in truth. In fact, Janet Auchincloss was determined that her daughter not repeat her mistake, and she undertook to make not only her future son-in-law aware of alcohol-addiction issues that destroyed her first marriage, but also his parents. She discussed this concern with Rose, asking her to share with Joe. The Catholic Church required mandatory marriage preparation for prospective brides and grooms who chose to marry in the Church. Consequently, both Jacqueline and Jack were properly disposed to accept one another until death, which would necessarily include both a "for better" and a "for worse".

Jackie Bouvier had a soul wound that JFK did not share. Her parents divorced when she was ten.[103] Divorce was a complicated, rare, legal proceeding at the time. In most states, the only available condition upon which the US courts would grant a valid divorce was with bona fides proof of adultery by the offending party. Divorce was socially frowned upon in New York society. Both Jacqueline and her younger sister Lee Bouvier learned to suffer silently for the rest of their lives as children of divorce.[104]

Anglican Catholic (Episcopalian in the US) Janet Auchincloss, Jacqueline's mother, had Irish and English roots. She counted among her ancestors the distinguished Lee family of Virginia. Jacqueline's wealthy New York father John Vernou Bouvier III, who owned an inherited, highly coveted seat on the New York Stock Exchange was strong, handsome, and dashing. His nickname was Black Jack, which was attributed to him because of his flamboyant lifestyle. A graduate of Phillips Exeter Academy who studied at Columbia University and graduated from Yale University's Sheffield Scientific School, his parents were New York attorney John Vernou Bouvier, Jr. and Maude Frances Sergeant. Black Jack was the eldest of their five children. After graduation from Yale, he worked at his dad's and uncle's stock brokerage firm, adding his name to the firm which then became known as Bouvier, Bouvier, and Bouvier. He was a hereditary member of the elite Maryland Society of the Cincinnati. Jack Bouvier's daughters Jacqueline, named for him and Lee, named for her mother, would be raised Christian in his Catholic denomination.[105]

The Kennedy family was reasonably well known at that time, especially by those who read the popular magazines of the day. They were frequently photographed and featured as upstanding Christian patriots. Glamorous photos of the various Kennedy children appeared in magazines most frequently during Joe Senior's appointment as US Ambassador to Great Britain. Rose Kennedy was a strong, independent woman who was greatly admired: she was considered a protype of the ideal Christian wife and mother of nine attractive, successful, patriotic children. Rose retained her trim figure and sparkling, twinkling blue eyes, properly coifed dark curly hair, and a smile that only the truly happy can muster. Her tall, handsome, athletic, financially successful husband Joe preferred that his wife wear the finest designer clothes of the seasons. Christians to their core, both Joe and Rose were always self-assured and confident of their calling, rooted as it was in the Catholic sacramental graces of holy matrimony.

The retired Boston mayor's daughter Rose, esteemed wife of the former American Ambassador to the ancient Court of Saint James in London and her husband Joe respected their son Jack's beautiful bride. They warmly welcomed lovely Jacqueline Bouvier into their family as a bonus daughter. JFK deeply appreciated that his exquisitely charming Catholic bride was a strong, sincere, kind-hearted, patriotic, intellectually savvy professional woman who was fully aware that, with God's help, a US Senator must serve his constituents. Jacqueline was a neophyte literary and artistic scholar who had studied at Miss Porters in Farmington, CT, Vassar, and in Paris at the Sorbonne. Like many educated, religiously cultivated Catholic women of her times, Jacqueline Bouvier entered marriage expecting to make whatever sacrifices necessary to bear John F. Kennedy's children and cooperate to the best of her ability on behalf of her husband's career. She was fully confident that Jack Kennedy had the moral strength to live his sacramental matrimonial commitments as he understood them.

Janet Auchincloss had always encouraged her Bouvier daughters to excel in whatever they did. She was elated that Jacqueline, from earliest childhood, shared her love for horses and helped her first born little daughter become an accomplished equestrienne. She was aware that Jackie had deeply admired John F. Kennedy's sacrificial, heroic service to the nation long before she met him. Janet recognized that her daughter was deeply in love with Senator John F. Kennedy, as he was with her. She hoped that their love for one another would carry them wherever fate's hand deigned. Like stalwart Rose and hard-working Joe Kennedy, Janet intended to be as helpful as possible to the newlyweds. And she was.

The mysterious, supernatural effects of sacramental matrimony sanctify the love of husband and wife, give them grace to bear with each other's weaknesses, and enable them to bring up their children in the fear and love of God.[106] Bridegroom Jack, deeply in love with his beautiful bride, notified his parents from his honeymoon in Acapulco, Mexico that his Jackie met his expectations. He cabled them saying: "At last, I know the true meaning of rapture. Jackie is enshrined forever in my heart. Thanks Mom and Dad for making me worthy of her. Your loving son, Jack."[107]

PART II

Freedom's Cost

"The winds with hymns of praise are loud,
Or low with sobs of pain,—
The thunder-organ of the cloud,
The dropping tears of rain.

With drooping head and branches crossed
The twilight forest grieves,
Or speaks with tongues of Pentecost
From all its sunlit leaves.

So, Nature keeps the reverent frame
With which her years began.
And all her signs and voices shame
The prayerless heart of man."[108]
—John Greenleaf Whittier

FOUR

Seeking the US Presidency

*Mankind must put an end to war
or war will put an end to mankind.*
—John F. Kennedy

The fierce anti-communist right wing of the Republican Party of the early 1950s had deep concerns about centrist President Eisenhower that he largely ignored. JFK, however, admired Eisenhower's predecessor President Franklin D. Roosevelt's ability to stimulate the latent idealism of the diverse American population, even in the dark days of recession and world war. FDR's style of leadership would influence Jack Kennedy's politics as he looked to the future.

JFK and his beautiful Jacqueline started out their married life in a large, riverfront home in McLean, Virginia, but their personal preferences soon led them to a townhouse in Georgetown. Jacqueline and Jack loved their N Street home that they noticed seemed to tilt just a bit to the right. As the young couple navigated through the early years of their marriage, Jacqueline felt called to audit a preeminent government course taught by esteemed Professor Jules Davids at Georgetown

University School of Foreign Service. Davids was renowned for his historical observation that every effectual generation in Western civilization exhibits a moral imperative to make the next generation better. With her fine mind and solid intellectual capacity, Jacqueline had perceived that her husband lived for a higher purpose than himself and she wanted to share the joy of that selfless higher resolve. She found cultural-historic stimulation in her class at the nearby university that Jacqueline enjoyed sharing with Jack and sometimes, even with her husband's dad. They, in turn, were delighted with Jacqueline's growing perceptions of contemporary issues emerging in various regions of the globe.

JFK was continuously plagued with medical problems. As his physical condition deteriorated, he chose to undergo yet another back surgery in 1954 to remove a severely infected back plate. Although Joe strenuously discouraged his second son from undertaking the dangerous surgery, JFK mysteriously knew that he could and would survive. One could ask: How did he know? Jack was admitted to the Hospital for Special Surgery in New York City on October 10, 1954. He had a few medical flareups that postponed his back surgery until 21 October. Unfortunately, and in spite of the finest care available, JFK developed a severe infection three days after his surgery and fell into a coma. As death appeared certain, a Catholic priest was summoned to again administer the healing Sacrament of the Sick known as Last Rites. Amazingly, Jack rallied. Some exclaimed that he literally rose from the dead.[109] It is not known if anyone inquired about the spiritual significance of this medical phenomenon. The surgery, however, left JFK with a gaping wound eight inches long that would not heal. Jacqueline cared for her suffering husband with kindness and tenderness beyond telling. Both she and her beloved Jack realized he faced a long, painful convalescence with many unforeseen twists and turns.

Two months after his challenging surgery, Jack was flown in his family's private plane to Palm Beach for Christmas, accompanied by his wife and care team. The senator could not walk or stand. Though Jack was mostly confined to his bed, with the ongoing prayers and encouragement of his family, he slowly began to heal. By February of 1955, as surgical complications became even more challenging, it became obvious that JFK would need to undergo yet another back surgery in New York. During that procedure, a spinal bone graft and removal of the metal plate were completed. Afterward, the senator and his wife returned to Palm Beach. During his second convalescence, with the loving help of his devoted Jackie, JFK began work on his second book, *Profiles in Courage*, which would ultimately receive a Pulitzer Prize.[110]

Jacqueline, still consumed with concern about her husband's fragile health in 1955, was pregnant with a little Kennedy baby whom she would unfortunately miscarry. Jack continued to experience serious side effects of his Addison's disease, and probably his undiagnosable Celiac's disease too. He suffered with constant headaches, stomach difficulties, respiratory infections, and relentless back pain.

In 1956, JFK was asked to give the televised nomination address at the democratic convention in Chicago. Adlai Stevenson was the Democratic candidate against hugely popular President "Ike" Eisenhower. Generously endowed with refined television skills, perhaps largely due to his father's vast Hollywood experience, JFK and his beautiful Jackie, who was expecting another Kennedy baby that year, were both introduced nationally to TV-viewing US voters at that time. Statistics had demonstrated that if Catholics in key election states who had voted for General Eisenhower in 1952 voted for JFK, he could win the presidency. This heretofore impossibility became the political goal of politically savvy Joe Kennedy. Jack knew his real enemy was time. It is not known if others around him, especially his wife, were aware of his limited lifespan. JFK was determined to accomplish his earth assignments with discipline and fealty to his "higher power," whom one can reasonably conjecture was Jesus Christ as revealed through the sacred deposit of faith of the Catholic denomination of the Christian Church worldwide.[111]

Jack Kennedy worked unremittingly during the 1956 democratic convention. Afterward, his health was so impaired that his mom and dad, after conferring with Jacqueline, insisted he escape relentless reporters and convalesce in the South of France with his vacationing family. In the last trimester of her second pregnancy, lovely, smiling Jacqueline Kennedy had found the ardors of the democratic convention to be terribly exhausting. Extremely tired, yet unable to travel abroad with her ailing husband, who was reticent to leave her side, she insisted upon joining her mother at her family seaside estate in Newport, Rhode Island to await the birth of their second child. The arrangement seemed ideal for both Jack and Jacqueline at the time. Reporters were relentless in pursuing them day and night, but paparazzi could not interfere at the Auchincloss Estate in Newport, or at Eden Roc in the South of France. Husbands were not permitted to be present at the birth of their children in the United States at that time and sickly Jack may have been considered an unnecessary liability to his wife and unborn child.

While vacationing at Eden Roc in the South of France with his family, who were deeply concerned about Jack's health, a few senate colleagues on holiday nearby chartered a luxury boat and invited JFK to join them. Jack loved the sea but had little patience with increased back pain that ocean turbulence can trigger unexpectedly on the high seas. A senate colleague was so relentless in insisting Jack join the group that he asked Joe for help. After consulting with Rose, Joe thought the mental health value for Jack boating on the beautiful Mediterranean Sea with a few supportive, intellectual friends was enticing. The entire family encouraged Jack to rouse himself and enjoy the cruise. Cautious Rose and Joe, always rightfully worried about JFK's precarious health, insisted that young Teddy accompany his older brother to look after him. They instructed Teddy to force Jack if necessary to rest, relax, and heal on their Mediterranean cruise. Rose and Joe had a long-established pattern of speaking by telephone nightly when they were apart.[112] Similarly, Jacqueline and Jack were able to communicate with each other during Jack's convalescence in the South of France; she too encouraged her weary husband to undertake the cruise, assuring him that she was well cared for at Newport. On August 23, 1956, however, Jacqueline unexpectedly hemorrhaged; she was transported by ambulance to the finest hospital in Newport where her stillborn daughter was delivered by emergency cesarean surgery. Though intercontinental transportation was often grueling in that era, Jack returned as quickly as possible to his weeping wife's bedside where the couple shared their grief over the loss of their stillborn daughter. Bereaved mother Jacqueline was slow to recover. She and Jack buried their little daughter (whom Jackie would tenderly refer to later in her life as her tiny Arabella) in the Catholic cemetery at Newport in a grave simply marked "daughter." This child's remains were later reinterred at Arlington National Cemetery where their stillborn daughter now rests with both her parents.[113]

* * *

Peering back through history's lens, one can see that by the 1800s, Czarist Russia was the largest country on earth. It extended from the Black Sea in Europe to the Bering Straits in the extreme east of Asia. Before the Russian revolution, Russia was a nation with a population of about 125 million predominantly illiterate people. By 1917, at least 85 percent were needy, always hungry peasants. The Russian language was the primary means of communication throughout the realm although only 44 percent were ethnically Russian. There were over 130 known nationalities within the empire; each had its own language and customs. Healthcare was practically nonexistent. Education was available only for the few elites in St. Petersburg or Moscow. Approximately 60 percent of all Russian males were totally illiterate. Most could not even sign their names. Scarce jobs available to them included manual labor or the military. There was little or no industry. Less than 13 percent of Russian females were able to read or write. There was no state-sponsored schooling. Peasants eked out a pitiful way of life tilling the harsh soil in the brutal climate of their fatherland. The backbreaking Russian agricultural system had changed little since the Middle Ages.[114]

In 1914, the ravages of war swept through Russia creating a burst of patriotism as soil-tilling male peasants were conscripted to defend their homeland. By 1915, Czar Nicholas II decided it was necessary to leave the management of his empire in the hands of his wife, the Empress Alexandra; he departed his palace to personally assume command of his Imperial Army. The war did not go well. Starving soldiers deserted; many simply disappeared or died along the way. Those who remained to fight were often weak, unprepared, and unpaid. The Tsarina Alexandra, mother of four daughters and one son, had been a German princess before her marriage to Czar Nicholas II. She was disliked throughout the Russian Empire as Germany was Russia's enemy at the time. During the sixteen-month absence of the Czar, his inexperienced wife is said to have appointed incompetent ministers who had little knowledge of how to govern the vast Russian Empire.[115]

Rumor laced with cruel gossip charged the Russian Empress with having fallen under the spell of a charlatan named Rasputin, said by some to be a man-demon who had emerged from the depths of hell to destroy the Russian nation and its people. Superstition apportioned to Rasputin, at best an opportunistic fake monk, mysterious powers of healing that allegedly delighted the pious Czarina. Her own survival, along with the Russian Empire's monarchial form of government were tied to her husband and their hemophilic heir, the child Aleksei Nikolayevich, born in 1904. Only male offspring of the Anointed Czar were authorized to govern Russia. During the Czar's absence, it is said that

Rasputin somehow convinced the Czarina that he had power to heal their hemophilic son and heir. There were no available means by which the Czarina could effectively communicate with her spouse about Rasputin's claims. Meanwhile, ambitious, power-hungry dissidents blamed Russia's extreme poverty and backwardness on Rasputin. In effect, Rasputin's alleged influence over the Russian Czarina became a means by which foreign revolutionaries, unwelcomed in the more stable courts of Europe, gained influence in Russia and demanded political change that would vastly benefit themselves.

As stirred-up mob protests among hungry peasant-surfs escalated throughout the massive Russian Empire, Rasputin became a political opportunity for non-Russian Marxist radicals to agitate illiterate, uneducated, starving Russian peasants who were so poor they had nothing to protect or lose. The Bolsheviks, a revolutionary political party grouped around Vladimir Lenin and Lev Davidovich Bronstein, better known as Leon Trotsky, demanded that real Russians rise up and cast off what Lenin called "a superstitious divine aura" prior generations had associated with the Russian Imperial Family.

Historically, as head of the Russian Orthodox Church, the Czar was perceived by the undereducated masses as an autocrat answerable only to the Highest Heavenly Power. By the second decade of the twentieth century, atheism became convenient for would-be leaders throughout the vast Russian Empire. Many of the inherent rights of man that flowed from atheist-driven Bolshevik organizers were actually shams by which they secretly planned to take over Russia's Imperil Government and its treasures for themselves. Bolsheviks would further enslave ignorant peasants, especially the greediest who were quickest to join their movement.[116] The starving Russian population unfortunately would effectively become voiceless cogs in the grinding wheels of atheistic Communism.

By December of 1917, Communist Russia established no-fault divorce whereby Orthodox sacramental marriage with divine love at the center was destroyed. Russian Communist women were required to work tirelessly for the state. Mothers were forced to place their children in state-run day care centers. By 1920, free abortion was legalized throughout the Soviet Russian State and was touted as patriotism. Effectively, family life died. Communist atheism became the glue that held Russia together as a nation. Russian Orthodox Church leadership was absorbed into the KGB. The secret police were charged with keeping order throughout the enormous Russian population. Religious worship was forbidden. Freedom of thought, word, or deed contrary to Communist atheism was nonexistent perhaps because it was so severely regulated and savagely punished. By 1937, Soviet Communism was identified in the West as a Satanic Scourge.

Between 1941 and 1945, cooperation between Great Britain, the US, and Soviets was deemed a politically necessary alliance to defeat the greater evil posed by Nazi Germany. US President Franklyn Delano Roosevelt lobbied Congress to allow the Soviet Union to participate in its Lend-Lease bill guaranteeing US economic war assistance. The remarkable military efforts of the Soviet Union on the Eastern Front allowed Great Britain and the United States to achieve a decisive military victory over Nazi Germany. But, at what cost to the Union of Soviet Socialist

Republics? Twenty-seven million Soviets died in the World War II conflict. Josef Stalin emerged as the thoroughly autocratic Communist Party leader of the remaining 170 million Soviet citizens in 1946. Extreme poverty remained a way of life throughout Russia. Gulags and concentration camps absorbed dissidents who failed to meet production quotas imposed by merciless Communist Party bureaucrats whose five-year plans were designed to bring the Soviet Union up to production standards commensurate with Western countries. To the shocking horror of many America leaders, by October of 1957, the Soviets successfully launched the first space satellite known as Sputnik 1. On May 1, 1960, an American U-2 spy plane was shot down over Russian territory and the pilot, Gary Powers was captured. The Russians used the badly traumatized pilot as a weapon to belittle the West.

JFK, with his beautiful, smiling wife Jacqueline, an icon of fashion, poise, and refinement, set out to win the hearts and committed votes of US citizens with the pivotal year 1960 set in his dad's political strategy. Family again brought strength to that goal. Young Bobby Kennedy, a World War II veteran, Harvard graduate, and competent attorney at law, quietly assumed control of his much-admired older brother's presidential campaign. Bobby's natural shrewdness, coupled with his highly developed interior life made RFK a formidable shadow leader. Big city political leaders of the day largely identified themselves as Irish Catholic Christians. Hesitant as they were to commit to one of their own, their support for John F. Kennedy cannot be overestimated. At the Democratic National Convention of 1960, the unthinkable happened. The great-grandson of poor, Irish

Catholic immigrants was nominated by the Democratic Party to run for President of the United States.

JFK's acceptance speech electrified the television viewing audience and invigorated the idealism of the young at heart who dared to aspire for personal greatness in sacrificial service to the needy. Campaign manager Bobby Kennedy made certain that the "neediest" of all was his older brother Jack waiting in the wings to fulfill his destiny in the land of liberty and justice for all. Inspired volunteers arrived in droves to open the new frontier that fearless, vigorous, valiant John F. Kennedy represented.

Republican Vice President and descendant of Yorba Linda California Quakers, Richard Milhouse Nixon was his formidable Republican Party opponent. Nixon had served in the navy in World War II and was honorably discharged as a lieutenant commander. A former congressman and senator, Nixon was an outspoken anti-communist. He was popular, well known nationally, and had enjoyed serving as Dwight D. Eisenhower's vice president for eight years. Soviet leadership, however, was unperturbed as the thoroughly Communist regime underestimated the US Democratic Party candidate, and perhaps even the outspoken anti-communist candidate of the Republican Party.

Shrewd American politicians feared there was hidden bigotry against Catholic Christians throughout the United States in 1960. That religious prejudice was largely based on ignorance of the religious components of ancient Christianity, which Catholicism espoused. In the pre-Vatican II era, a few American voters were concerned that illiterate Catholics took orders directly from the Pope, or from their local Catholic hierarchy. Elite, Harvard-educated world traveler, and bona fides war hero John F. Kennedy was by now a formidable communicator who would prove himself a worthy Catholic Christian political leader in the presidential campaign of 1960. Jack Kennedy was not known to squander opportunities.

JFK's health problems had rightfully taught him valuable lessons in leadership, the first of which was to master himself. Perhaps ahead of his political times, JFK developed mental conditioning techniques that allowed him to effectively rise above his personal difficulties and laser-focus on specific issues. Those close to him watched in amazement as Kennedy successfully recalibrated his central nervous system, leaving his crutches hidden in his vehicle as he sprinted to speaking engagements, glad-handed eager voters, and hugged elderly folks who had queued for hours hoping to meet the affirming senator from Massachusetts. JFK had befriended his disabilities. No one would see weakness in the courageous, indomitable Democratic Party candidate for the presidency of the United States.[117]

Jack Kennedy had advantages that Nixon did not. He was educated among elites at Harvard and Stanford where he networked with America's brightest youths, heard their dreams, and shared their brilliant idealism in spite of the horror of human combat he endured in World War II. Nixon had served as vice president with highly popular General Eisenhower who began and ended his two-term presidency as a war hero beloved of his constituents. Richard Nixon, a Duke Law School graduate, had war experience, political connections, and education, but little personal charisma.

Jack Kennedy genuinely admired history's great leaders whose rhetoric had inspired the masses with confidence and sacrifice in the worst of times. He understood leadership. Some attribute Kennedy's political acumen to his handicaps that required constant personal discipline. Others ascribe his admirable skills to the social opportunities he experienced in personal contact with diplomatic peers in the embassies of the world. More importantly perhaps: he was a surviving World War II war hero whose hands-on leadership was highly tested in self-sacrificing service in the bloody South Pacific. There are even those who ascribe John F. Kennedy's more patrician attributes to his highly developed but hidden soul strength refined over a lifetime of lonely, painful, physical rehabilitations drenched in surrender to the mercy of Divine Providence.

Victory required Massachusetts Senator John F. Kennedy, as candidate for US President in 1960, to choose a running mate. Expediency revealed that Lyndon B. Johnson of Texas, a giant in the US Senate, would be most helpful by attracting the most needed votes in southern states. The Kennedy-Johnson alliance was forged out of necessity. Johnson had outspoken animosity toward Kennedy whom he considered an elite Catholic New Englander. Lyndon Johnson's prejudices were somewhat disguised in ways perceptive politicians and the lens of history recognize. The popular, long-time Democratic Speaker of the House of Representatives, Sam Rayburn, knew Senate Majority Leader Lyndon Johnson well. He also knew Jack Kennedy and Richard Nixon. Raeburn had no reservations about instructing Lyndon Johnson: "I am a wiser man . . . Besides, that other fella [Nixon] called me a traitor, and I don't want a man who calls me a traitor to be President of the United States. We've got to beat him, and you've got to do everything you can to help."[118]

JFK believed Lyndon Johnson was a man of force and decision to whom the government could be responsibly consigned, should the hand of fate shorten JFK's presidential days. Patriotic Lyndon Johnson accepted the second place behind Kennedy as vice presidential nominee on the Democratic ticket.

Eighty thousand people gathered in the Los Angeles Coliseum to hear Rose and Joe Kennedy's second son, Jacqueline's husband, and Caroline's dad accept the Democratic Party nomination for US President. Everyone there heard John F. Kennedy's luminescent imperative that no man can thwart: "The world has been close to war before—but now man, who has survived all previous threats to his existence, has taken into his mortal hands the power to exterminate the entire species some seven times over ... But I believe the times demand invention, innovation, imagination, decision. I am asking each of you to be new pioneers on that new frontier."[119]

* * *

Three days before the presidential election of 1960, a Gallop poll disclosed a dead heat. Kennedy was leading by 50.5 percent to Nixon's 49.5 percent. This election was too close to decipher. At the start of the campaign, some journalists had complained that both senators were cut from the same cloth, part of the Fraternity Row crowd.[120] By November, there was a distinct difference that journalists observed between the two candidates for the highest office in the land. "Nixon, who had started out projecting an image of calm, of maturity; the dignity of the experienced statesman had become angry and grim. A posture of indignation had replaced the earlier quiet chatty manner."[121] It was not yet Nixon's time. A *New York Times* journalist noted: "The crowds tensed him [Nixon] up. I watched him ball his fists, set his jaw, hurl himself stiff-legged to the barriers at the airport and begin shaking hands. He was wound up like a watch spring . . . No ease."[122]

By contrast, Charles Kuralt of CBS observed the change in the two candidates. He mentioned the relaxed, smiling JFK—who had presented in summer as a serious man who earlier had seemed cold and efficient. Historian Robert Daller said: "It was as if running against someone as humorless and possibly ruthless as Nixon strengthened Kennedy's faith in himself—in the conviction not only that he would be a better president but the energy to get the job done could come not just from within, and not just from family dynamics, but from the sea of American faces that smiled when he [smilingly] stepped toward them."[123] That was the sign JFK wanted—a recognition that he was truly called to the presidency for a higher purpose than himself. The war hero who attributed his heroism in the South Pacific to circumstances beyond his control—"They sank my boat"—was following the invisible hand of fate—that Kennedy had learned was foolish to question. And so, as the campaign for the presidency progressed, JFK simply surrendered to totally mysterious Divine Providence whose ways few leaders ever penetrate. His "surrender" meant that it was up to John F. Kennedy to do his utmost for His Highest as he perceived his moral duty.

Bigotry against the ancient church of Rome had been a troubling problem throughout the campaign that JFK understood was steeped in misinformation. His knowledge of history, particularly of the inspirational, seemingly divinely ordained work of the founders of the American Republic, inspired Kennedy to set the record straight for those who may have misunderstood the US Constitution and Bill of Rights. He believed that those to whom much is given, much is expected.[124] And so, JFK asked his staff to arrange a televised address to pierce the very heart of religious darkness with truth. His campaign scheduled a televised address before formidable Protestant religious leaders. Kennedy's famous US political speech outlining the freedom of religion clause of the US Constitution by the World War II veteran who was highly educated in the school of hard knocks, as well as *cum laude* from Harvard University was delivered to fellow patriots of the Greater Houston Ministerial Association on September 12, 1960.

FIVE

Leadership

> *... [T]here can be no doubt that,
> if all nations could refrain from interfering
> in the self-determination of others,
> the peace would be much assured."*
> —John F. Kennedy

Senator John F. Kennedy, a skilled television personality, was photogenic and genteel by nature. He was considered by the viewing public as manly but gracious, a polished gentleman war hero in the American tradition of heroes of yesteryear. After JFK's Houston speech, the Catholic Christian denomination ceased to be an electoral stumbling block among the educated voting public of the United States. Richard Nixon, however, was indeed a formidable opponent who made a few largely unnoticed though costly mistakes in his political strategy. Henry Cabot Lodge of Massachusetts, who had been appointed by President Eisenhower as US Ambassador to the United Nations became Nixon's running mate. JFK and Nixon were offered an opportunity to participate in prime-time television debates, the first of their kind in the early days of television broadcasting.

Both candidates accepted. Dick Nixon felt confident believing that he was a better debater than Jack Kennedy. The scheduled and highly publicized debates took place in an empty studio in autumn of 1960. The mutually agreed topics were domestic and foreign policy. Unfortunately, Richard Nixon had been sick preceding the debates, but he refused to cancel free publicity. Although he had lost weight, his busy campaign schedule and natural frugality precluded shopping for better fitting clothes. Consequently, he appeared on television with swollen eyes, sagging jowls and ill-fitting garments, a political error that severely impacted voter confidence in Richard Nixon. John F. Kennedy was an expert at the television medium of communication. He had prepared for the debates by relaxing at his family home in Palm Beach, Florida. The contrast between Nixon's ailing pallor, coupled with his obvious discomfort in front of television cameras, and Kennedy's healthy suntan and relaxed demeanor resulted in a public opinion tie, foretelling a photo finish among probable voters in the November election.

JFK and his siblings were raised by Joe and Rose Kennedy to care about and for the less fortunate. In late October of 1960, pregnant Coretta King was worried that her husband, Reverend Doctor Martin Luther King Jr. would be lynched while serving an unjust four-month prison sentence at hard labor. Famous baseball legend Jackie Robinson pleaded with Richard Nixon for help, but Nixon refused. JFK's sister Eunice, speaking for her entire family, insisted publicly that something be done to help the King family. Jack Kennedy was aware of mortal danger to unborn children whose mothers suffer trauma and phoned Mrs. King, comforting her and promising his help. In spite of heavy political criticism, JFK arranged for his younger brother Bobby to obtain bail and the immediate release of Reverend Doctor Martin Luther King, Jr. Mrs. King never forgot the political kindness of both Bobby and Jack Kennedy. She would remember that Reverend Dr. King too never forgot.

On election night, Kennedy had a hint that he might win if the hand of fate whom he knew as Divine Providence so deigned. When poll results lagged into the early morning hours, exhaustion claimed him, and he slept soundly. He could rest knowing he had done his utmost to win the presidency. By morning, it was clear that forty-three-year-old John F. Kennedy was narrowly elected thirty-fifth president of the United States. The date was November 9, 1960. He did not know, nor did it matter to him that he would have only three years and thirteen days left on earth to serve his country. Envy has many faces; malicious rumors that JFK's family money bought the election proliferate, even into the modern day.[125] "Such accusations were impossible to prove."[126] Outgoing President Eisenhower was widely quoted as having remarked that his vice president, Richard Nixon, lost the 1960 election for his failure to help the Reverend Doctor Martin Luther King Jr. family. There are many reasons scholars continue to investigate the grandeur of American voting patterns, especially those evident in the Nixon-Kennedy election of 1960. No one could demonstrate significant fraud anywhere. At the time, none seems to have consulted the Bible that assures there is a time for everything.[127] The winds of Divine Providence are subtle but always prevailing.

Theodore H. White in his best-selling, Pulitzer Prize-winning book *The Making of the President 1960* wrote that "this margin of popular vote (in 1960) is so thin as to be, in all reality, nonexistent. If only 4500 voters in Illinois and 28000 voters in Texas changed their minds, the sum of their 32,000 votes would have moved both these states, with their combined fifty-one electoral votes, into the Nixon column."[128]

Thomas Reeves opined in his book *A Question of Character*: "In eleven states, a shift of less than 1 percent of the vote would have switched the state's electoral votes." Although conscious (and unconscious) racial, social, political, and religious prejudices too often cling to the fabric of some segments of American life, voter tastes are so varied that no one really knows exactly what stimulates a majority of Americans to go to the polls to vote for the candidate of their choice on election day. In the final analysis, it was concluded that "however close, Kennedy's victory represented the will of the electorate ... Whatever gains and losses John Kennedy's presidency might have brought to the country and the world, his election of 1960 marked a great leap forward in religious tolerance that has served the nation well ever since."[129]

Looking again through the lens of history at the presidential election of John F. Kennedy in 1960, many laud his memory when reminiscing about his idealism and sacrificial commitment to duty. Unfortunately, however, from the beginning of John F. Kennedy's actual candidacy for the presidency, disturbed people openly spoke out against him. As political negativity engendered more negativity, malcontents increased internationally. But there were significant others who admired him. Among them, presidential historian Arthur Schlesinger, Jr. admitted that "Kennedy, of course, was our Harvard and Massachusetts senator. More important, we found ourselves, as we saw more of him, bound to him by increasingly strong ties of affection and respect."[130]

Many notables remembered Jack Kennedy from his youth when his dad was American Ambassador to the Court of Saint James. Among them was JFK's good friend William David Ormsby-Gore, Fifth Baron Harlech, a member of the English House of Lords, born on May 18, 1918, and a year younger than JFK. He spoke fondly of his experiences with Jack Kennedy, and his many personal visits with the Kennedy family in Hyannis Port. Historian Schlesinger, Jr. wrote about his own first visit to Hyannis Port: ". . . [Jack] Kennedy called from Hyannis Port to invite me for dinner that night. This was my first visit to the Kennedy compound; and though I had met Jacqueline Kennedy several times since their marriage, it was really the first occasion for a leisurely chat with her. My wife was not able to come, and there were only the three of us . . . Jack in a tweed jacket, sweater and slacks, hatless and tieless, swinging a cane and looking fit and jaunty, and Jacqueline, her hair slightly blown in the breeze, glowing in beauty [from their walk on the dunes]. One could only think: What a wildly attractive young couple. It took another minute to remember that this was the President-elect of the United States and his wife. Jacqueline was reading *Remembrance of Things Past* when I arrived. In the course of the evening, I realized that, underneath a veil of lovely inconsequence, she concealed tremendous awareness, an all-seeing eye, and a ruthless judgment. As for Kennedy . . . I was struck by the impersonality of his attitudes and his readiness to see the views and interests of others. I was also a little surprised by the animation and humor of his assessment of people and situations . . .

[his] easy and casual wit, turned incisively and impartially on himself and his rivals were one of his most beguiling qualities, as those who had known him longer had understood for years."[131]

Another influential personage was Philip Graham, a brilliant graduate of Harvard Law School, former law clerk for Supreme Court Justice Frankfurter, and a combat veteran who served in World War II in the Far East. After the war, he became publisher and editor of the popular *Washington Post* daily newspaper owned by his father-in-law Eugene Meyer. Phil Graham made the *Washington Post* the keystone in an ever-increasing newspaper conglomerate. A man of undoubtable substance, Graham, was "captivated by Kennedy's candor, detachment and intellectual force."[132]

It was well known that President-elect John F. Kennedy believed a strong military is the best defense against aggression. His first best-selling book *Why England Slept* had laid out his personal observations about governments that ignore their surrounding enemies' expensive military buildups. When his father served as US Ambassador in London, Harvard student John F. Kennedy had met the British Prime Minister Neville Chamberlain who mistakenly thought he had brokered a peace deal with Hitler. His famous statement, "I have brought peace to our times" proved to be wishful thinking. Unfortunately, Chamberlain had not recognized that the stronger a nation's military, the more likely it would succeed in negotiations with potential enemies. Kennedy would not make that mistake.

Nuclear bombs dropped on Hiroshima and Nagasaki that ended World War II changed the trajectory of global war and international diplomacy forever. The East-West confrontation that resulted from the final settlement of the Second World War at Yalta left the Soviet block of nations with nuclear weapons of mass destruction that would ensure Russian "first strike" capacity. The US became the presumed protector of European NATO countries as well as the American homeland. Dwight D. Eisenhower had served as Supreme Commander of the Allied Expeditionary Force in Western Europe and at the war's conclusion united the member-nations of NATO. He was elected and served as US President from 1952 until 1960 when John F. Kennedy assumed the reigns of the young United States.

British Ambassador to the United States David Ormsby-Gore, a long-time personal friend of both Jack and Bobby Kennedy, was commissioned in 1939 into the Royal Artillery Regiment, served in the "Phantom" reconnaissance unit, and worked with airborne and other special units. At the war's conclusion, he held the rank of major on the general staff. Kennedy personally requested that David be appointed British ambassador to the US. Though Ormsby-Gore worked well with England's Prime Minister Harold Macmillan, he was a true confident of both Jack and Bobby Kennedy who referred to him as their kind of ambassador. At a time when many high-placed, respectably educated survivors of World War II had strong opinions about the folly of war, conservative Ormsby-Gore was no exception. He and Macmillan would be instrumental in pushing forth a Nuclear Test Ban Treaty with the Russians that had failed for a decade before Ormsby-Gore and JFK would succeed [in 1963].

JFK's approach to foreign policy was realistic and pragmatic. He realized that he was the servant of America's magnificent ideals. Beneath the glitter of his life and office, beneath the casual exterior of the determined politician, "was a good and decent man with a conscience that told him what was right and a heart that cared about the well-being of those around him."[133] Kennedy had observed the strategies of the Eisenhower era from his Senate seat and appreciated the skill and wisdom of Secretary of State John Foster Dulles and his brother Allen Dulles who headed the CIA during the 1950s. Jack also knew and appreciated Secretary Dulles's son Avery, a Jesuit priest and colleague of eminent Catholic theologian John Courtney Murray SJ. Murray's skillful constitutional law research allowed him to comfortably reconcile ancient Roman Catholic Christianity with brilliant religious pluralism guaranteed in the politically advanced US system of government. Murray's work at the Second Vatican Council was essential in the formulation of the Council's Declaration on Religious Liberty, *Dignitatis Humanae*.

In November of 1961, JFK was aware that many in Washington, especially those who remained loyal to Eisenhower's vice president, Richard Nixon, were troubled by his presidential victory. Joe Kennedy Senior was sorely disappointed by the slim margin of victory his second son garnered in the general election of 1960. He had worked hard and spent lavishly only to discover "First, I thought he [JFK] would get a bigger Catholic vote than he did. Second, I did not think so many would vote against him because of his religion."[134] In fact, University of Michigan political scientists concluded that the religious issue was the "strongest single factor overlaid on basic partisan loyalties in the 1960 election."[135] Although Kennedy had received a minority of Protestant votes, Jewish and Black voters supported him in large enough numbers to win the presidency by the narrowest margin in American history. But victory is always victory, even when the margins are slim.

* * *

During JFK's presidency, Washington DC had the flavor of small-town USA, especially in the Georgetown neighborhoods where everyone seemed to know everyone else, and cave dwellers did not care who was politically important from year to year.[136] The District of Columbia was humid and hot during three seasons and air conditioning was rare in the early1960s. If snow fell in winter, it usually melted within hours. Street cars rattled along the ancient cobblestone streets, and Sugars on Thirty-fifth Street was a drug-store meeting place for those who sought a quick coffee or sugar-laced soft drinks that flowed from spouts over crushed ice. Hilltop and Tehans were dining places across the street from the Walsh Building at Georgetown University that attracted hungry luncheon crowds. The Georgetown University Shop on the corner catered to discriminating men and Georgetown University's mostly male students who desired to purchase fine apparel.

In the early morning hours of inauguration day on January 20, 1961, rarely seen snow shrouded Washington, DC in high drifts everywhere, crippling all street traffic. A Georgetown University student observed that as most people slept in the eerie dawn silence, John F. Kennedy, the newly elected US President, accompanied by a few secret service agents, crept into a side pew of Holy Trinity parish church on Thirty-sixth Street in Georgetown for the early morning Mass. Perhaps unbeknown to the President-elect, his mother, true to her life commitment, was already worshipping alone in a nearby pew. The media were undoubtedly unaware; weary reporters had covered a glamorous inaugural gala hosted by Joe Kennedy that did not end until the President-elect departed at four o'clock that morning. Although both Rose and Jacqueline had retired early, Rose walked at first light to Holy Trinity parish church along the snow-cleared streets. Unfortunately, little is publicly known about JFK's personal interior life. His Dad publicly adjured his children: "Never, ever wear your religion publicly." No one knows if mother and son were informed of each other's presence on that auspicious inauguration day that no public transportation was available in Washington due to the unusually heavy snowfall. To this day, however, scholars can agree that the First Amendment of the US Constitution is a beacon of light that safeguards the underlying strength of the United States and its ever-growing, highly pluralistic population.

> "Congress shall make no law respecting an establishment of religion or prohibiting the free exercise thereof: or abridging the freedom of speech, or of the press; or the right of the people peaceably to assemble."

* * *

What is somewhat known is the observable spiritual path Rose Kennedy undertook on behalf of her husband and children. She remembered in her later years:

> "Faith, I would tell them, is a great gift from God and is a living gift, to sustain us in our lives on earth, to guide us in our activities, to be a source of solace and comfort, so we should do everything we can to strengthen its roots, to nourish it, and to help it to grow and flourish, and try never to lose it. Religion was never oppressive or even conspicuous in our household, but it was always there, part of our lives, and the Church's teachings and customs were observed. We went to Mass on Sundays, holy days, First Fridays. We said grace before meals... [We would ask our children] Why did Jesus accept crucifixion and suffer and die for us? What was he doing for us, and by example telling all of us?"[137]

* * *

Savants of all generations assert that directed prayers of parents for one another and for their children are never in vain. All prayers, even if they are feeble or begrudged, allow divine love to flow to any person, situation or project.

JFK, an undisputed student of history, was heard to say, "Those who don't know history condemn themselves to repeat its mistakes." He may have been aware of the apocryphal story of Hindu freedom fighter Mahatma Gandhi's observation: "If Christians lived their faith, everyone would be Christian." No one really knows how Rose Kennedy expressed her personal religious beliefs with words to her husband and children, but she was outwardly active in living her faith and expected them to do so also. Rose said: "Faith in God and His wisdom and mercy and goodness and in the teachings of the Church had been instilled in me from my earliest years."[138]

On inauguration day, Rose and Joe were overjoyed at the refinement their son and his beautiful wife were capable of representing to the world on behalf of the United States. Both of Jack Kennedy's parents, along with Jacqueline's mother Janet Auchincloss, were delighted that JFK, and his lovely Jacqueline were willing to serve their country so selflessly. Jackie's mom was relieved that her daughter was so happy in spite of her recent caesarian surgery in late November.[139] These enlightened parents, each in their own ways, had sacrificially taught their children the value of service by their personal examples.

Joe Senior valued his immortal soul enough to include Reverend John J. Cavanaugh, a Catholic priest of the Congregation of the Holy Cross and retired President of Notre Dame University as his close personal friend, spiritual advisor and traveling companion. He was driven to provide for his wife and each of his nine children in ways that would never force them to enter the world of commerce simply to find food and shelter, freeing them to serve others not so fortunate. Why? Because he could. He and Rose welcomed each child as a gift from God and with proper training, which was their duty to impart, a future citizen of the Heavenly Kingdom. They were determined to do their part to support their children's eternal salvation. Each Kennedy child, in his or her own way, learned that the purpose of life on earth is to experience the unique gospel journey all humans travel, often through dark valleys seething with cobwebs of death, but ever onward with Christ to Eternal Bliss.[140] The wind blows where it will. Not so for humans born on earth into situated freedom. Baptismal faith assured the First Family and their elders that the invisible Holy Spirit, personally accessed through prayer, lifts believers closer to the illuminated gospel path of Jesus Christ. As the US Founders had prophesied, Kind Providence never fails.

In Rose Kennedy's memoirs she remembered: ". . . At Easter, we asked the meaning of the Resurrection [of Jesus] and life everlasting . . . [Our children memorized their] Catechism: I would hear them recite their lessons every week . . ."[141] There were many blessings for families of those times where the Baltimore Catechism was taught and lived. It contained simple reasons for human existence and earth duties. The most basic examples include:

Q. Who made the world?

A. God made the world.

Q. Who is God?

A. God is the Creator of Heaven and earth and of all things.

Q. What is [a human]?

A. [A human] is a creature composed of body and soul and made in the image and likeness of God.

Q. Is this likeness in the body or in the soul?

A. This likeness is chiefly in the soul.

Q. How is the soul like to God?

A. The soul is like to God because it is a spirit that will never die and has understanding and free will.

Q. Why did God make you?

A. God made me to know Him, to love Him, and to serve Him in this world, and to be happy with Him forever in the next.

Q. Of which must we take more care, our soul or our body?

A. We must take more care of our soul than of our body.

Q. Why must we take more care of our soul than of our body?

A. We must take more care of our soul than of our body, because in losing our soul we lose God and everlasting happiness.

Q. What must we do to save our souls?

A. To save our souls, we must worship God by faith, hope, and charity; that is, we must believe in Him, hope in Him, and love Him with all our heart.

Q. How shall we know the things which we are to believe?

A. We shall know the things which we are to believe from the catholic church, through which God speaks to us.

Q. Where shall we find the chief truths which the catholic church teaches?

A. We shall find the chief truths which the catholic church teaches in the Apostles' Creed.[142]

* * *

Given the abominable weather conditions in Washington, DC on Inauguration Day 1960, Rose's knowledge of her second son's medical issues, and somewhat aware of the far-reaching gravity of her son's forthcoming leadership responsibilities may have led her to walk the snow-covered roads of Georgetown to Mass on that most intriguing day. But Rose denied any concern for her son saying that daily Mass was her custom. Posterity has John F. Kennedy's Inaugural Address to reflect upon the newly elected US President's reason for beginning his short presidency worshipping God alone and as unobtrusively as possible at morning Mass at Holy Trinity parish church in Georgetown.

Beginning in JFK's early days in the US Senate, Ted Sorensen had worked closely with Jack. He knew Kennedy better than most and observed that JFK was not a snob; he was balanced, disciplined, and practical. Sorensen, a Nebraska Quaker, said of the millionaire Ivy League President-elect that he "loved sports, pop music, and movies; he had suffered injury and endured family tragedy; he had a wonderful sense of humor and a deep love of family."[143] The thirty-fifth US President and his beautiful wife Jacqueline were parents of nearly two-month-old John F. Kennedy, Jr. and three-year-old Caroline. Family and staff were all busy preparing the young family to move from their N Street residence in Georgetown to the White House on Inauguration Day. At noon, shivering notables bundled in their warmest clothes filled the inaugural stage as the young US President-elect stood without coat or hat to take his Presidential Oath of Office. Television cameras showed the Chief Justice of the US Supreme Court, Earl Warren, administering the Oath of Office to Jack Kennedy who affirmed his Presidential Oath with his outstretched hand resting on an old Fitzgerald family Bible. The global television audience viewed the US transfer of power from two-term President and World War II Supreme Commander of Allied Forces in Europe, Dwight D. Eisenhower to a younger generation represented by forty-three-year-old John F. Kennedy.

JFK strived to make the best of the allotted time he would have on earth. Having already lost two of his dear siblings, he could never forget a noted physician in London who had informed him years earlier that his lifespan probably would be forty-five years at best. No one knows if JFK endured a near-death experience that is part of the popular culture of modern times when he received the Last Rites of the Catholic Church on four occasions. During his presidency, Kennedy would assure his local Washington, DC auxiliary bishop Philip Hannan that he would never, under any circumstances, compromise his immortal soul.[144] Significantly, JFK prayed daily on his knees that his actions would never compromise the spiritual or material welfare of others.[145] JFK could never forget that he, his wife, and their children were descendants of once hungry, struggling immigrants. Consequently, he had a lifelong interest in questions of social justice.[146] Kennedy highly respected the policies of Pope Saint John XXIII and resonated deeply with his Encyclical *Pacem in Terris*.[147]

Journalist David Talbot presciently observed a vigorous new muscularity in JFK's international policy: "If the new president was committed to expanding America's nuclear arsenal, he was even more determined never to use it. This seemingly contradictory position was vividly displayed in Kennedy's ringing inaugural address. The speech revealed a man with 'one foot in the Cold War, and one foot in a new world he saw coming'. With its double-edge message of bellicose vigilance and pacific idealism, the speech appealed to a broad political spectrum."[148]

Generations remain reassured that the inaugural address of John F. Kennedy, much of which he wrote himself, reveals who the thirty-fifth US President was and what he intended to accomplish in his thousand-day presidency. The new President looked directly into the televised lens of history as he spoke his immortal fourteen-minute inaugural address for all times and governments and peoples longing for life, liberty, and the pursuit of happiness. As nations continue to aspire to the light-filled policy of that speech, the divine mystery of peace on earth lifts one person at a time.

SIX

From Crisis to Crisis

*"A war today or tomorrow . . .
would not be like any war in history."*
—John F. Kennedy[149]

Contemporary political commentator Michael Knowles mused: "Whether or not a political system 'works' depends on what it's working toward. Socialism strives to tear down traditional society. At that task, socialism has succeeded everywhere it has been tried, at least for a time. The problem with socialism isn't the inefficiency; it's the evil. Marx did not set out to tinker with markets and redistribute some wealth. He sought to radically transform society by changing human nature. He hated religion because he opposed God, the author of human nature. He sided with Satan, as he confessed in letters and ghoulish poetry . . ."[150]

Soviet Premier Nikita Khruschev had a stronghold on power in winter of 1961. Surprisingly, he was so delighted with young JFK's inaugural address that he personally undertook to have the entire speech printed in the Communist propaganda newspaper *Pravda*.[151] Outgoing President Eisenhower believed he had warned JFK that Khruschev and his military hardliners had effectively taken control of Cuba, a tiny island ninety miles from Florida. He said their puppet was Fidel Castro. Eisenhower may have expected JFK to support CIA activities in the Western Hemisphere, especially in and around Cuba.

John F. Kennedy was a religious man, a Christian who nobly honored his faith traditions as unobtrusively as circumstances permitted. He was aware that evil stalks the highways and byways of earth's dark valleys looking for prey.[152] Presidential historian Arthur Schlesinger, Jr., who worked closely with JFK in his administration wrote that: "Kennedy was called an intellectual very seldom before 1960 and very often thereafter . . . He was a man of action who could pass easily over to the realm of ideas and confront intellectuals with perfect confidence in his capacity to hold his own . . . His mind . . . had its own salient qualities—it was objective, practical, ironic, skeptical, enfettered, and insatiable."[153] Kennedy was also quite confident that wherever there is light, there is hope.[154]

Representing the Greatest Generation, JFK was aware that only a fool would think that every nation be marked as either Communist or anti-Communist, or even be interested in the Cold War. Kennedy knew that neutralism had been part of United States history for over a hundred years, and he regarded its practice by many struggling nations as inevitable. Jack Kennedy expected other nations would not respect American views, but he sincerely believed they would inevitably support their own freedom. Consequently, he based his foreign policy on that belief.

* * *

JFK exhibited a patriotic sense of pride and excitement about living in the White House, steeped as it was in the history of those who had preceded him. "On his second full day in office, returning from Mass with Paul Fay and his brother Teddy, he invited them in for an inspection; and sitting in the only chair in the still bare and nearly empty oval office, he spun around . . ."[155] That week, he and Jacqueline took guests on a White House tour with their dear friend Franklin Roosevelt Jr. asking him the history of a particular room as they passed through. Economist John Kenneth Galbraith, an accomplished diplomat and distinguished author whom JFK would soon appoint ambassador to India, recalled that Kennedy had complained that the White House furnishings included too many reproductions.[156]

Jacqueline would soon delight her husband with her skilled research and her restoration and replacement of reproductions with original furnishings within the White House. She would form a fine arts committee to raise funds for the project with the help of Rachel (Bunny) Mellon, Henry DuPont, Dorthy (Sister) Parish and Stephany Boudin. Jacqueline would enjoy overseeing the restoration of selected rooms of the White House to their nineteenth-century splendor. Sharing her husband's long view of history, she would be instrumental in creating a White House Historical Association to maintain its artwork and furnishings in perpetuity. By 1962, Mrs. Kennedy would explain in her quiet, refined voice the history and beauty of the restored interiors of the White House to a global television audience. She would realize soon enough that the three years she spent in the White House would be the "happiest time of my life. It was when we (she and JFK) were the closest."[157]

Though he was younger, and his health was more compromised than most world leaders, JFK expended immense effort in surrounding himself with the best and brightest people of his times. "For seventy-two days preceding his inauguration, Jack had worked with Eisenhower on an orderly transfer of power, with Nixon on a restoration of national unity, with Democratic leaders on reshaping the National Committee, and with his own aides on handling all the administrative problems of the transition period, including finances, transportation, accommodations, press relations and attention to the enormous number of letters pouring in from heads of state, well-wishers, job-seekers, old friends and myriad others..."[158] His inspiring personal discipline was obvious: Jack missed only one day of work in his thousand days as US President. He appointed his trusted younger brother Bobby Kennedy as attorney general. Both men realized that they stood in the shadows of some of the world's greatest leaders. Effective trailblazers don't forget the sacrifices of heroes of the past, and especially of President Eisenhower who had publicly warned before leaving office that the nation's military leaders tend to forge alliances with entities that supply the instruments of war. With the virulent spread of freedom-sapping Communism among emerging nations, containment had been Eisenhower's militarily enforced foreign policy.

World traveler JFK had highly tuned sensitivity to the plight of struggling populations not only in the US, but globally. Coupled with that sensitivity was his unshakable confidence that the US Republic is the best form of government yet achieved by humankind. Though frequent medically prescribed swimming and extensive use of a rocking chair were necessary for his pain management, Kennedy intended to protect and defend all the citizens of the United States along with others throughout the world seeking freedom to pursue an honorable life steeped in liberty.[159]

JFK's policy outlook was remarkable for a leader of his times. Representing those who had served in World War II, he was keenly aware of the extraordinary value of travel and education to illumine responsibility to help the downtrodden work their way out of hunger, pernicious superstition, and malevolence. Believing that untold numbers of educated American youths were willing to sacrifice their time and talent to assist suffering people on other shores, Kennedy enthusiastically supported formation of the Peace Corps under the leadership of his brother-in-law Sargent Shriver. This new agency aimed to provide an opportunity for dedicated Americans to serve their country and help make the world a better place for multitudes. Young Americans heard the call in JFK's inaugural address in 1961: "Ask not what your country can do for you. Ask what you can do for your country." Huge numbers stepped forward and continue to do so.

Peace Corps volunteers undergo intense training and serve in developing countries struggling with poverty, illiteracy, and disease. In modern times, 900 young Americans serve in forty-seven countries around the world. Since JFK signed Executive Order 10924, establishing the Peace Corps on March 1, 1961, and Congressional legislation on September 22, 1961, authorizing and funding the Peace Corps, more than 235,000 Peace Corps volunteers have served in 141 countries. 309 sacrificed their lives. Peace Corps volunteers understand that even with their limited, or nonexistent local linguistic and cultural skills, they will work in unfamiliar environments doing their best to improve local conditions. Considered one of the most prestigious international programs available to educated young American citizens, the Peace Corps is an all-volunteer organization powered by hands-on service. Less the 25 percent of those who apply are accepted. Peace Corps volunteers choose the country in which they will serve, the work they will perform, and the length of time they will serve. Some of their projects include constructing roads, developing water and sewage systems, improving farming methods, providing basic medical care, and teaching the illiterate. The median age for college-educated Peace Corps volunteers is twenty-eight. Numerous nongovernmental and humanitarian not-for-profit organizations have grown out of the Peace Corps. These NGOs are staffed primarily with young Americans who are willing to live abroad and serve the less fortunate. Their goal is to make a significant difference in the lives of others struggling with poverty, illiteracy, and disease.

Ten days after his prescient inaugural address, JFK rendered his televised State of the Union address to the joint session of Congress. Warning that life would not be easy for US citizens in the 1960s, he courageously counseled the Congress and his vast TV audience: "The hopes of all mankind rest upon us, not simply upon those of us in this chamber, but upon the peasant in Laos, the fisherman in Nigeria, the exile from Cuba, the spirit that moves every man and nation who share our hopes for freedom and the future."

Pressing US economic difficulties, and Communist China's global ambitions coupled with Russian military aggression, especially in the developing nations of the Western Hemisphere, were among the most difficult problems JFK faced as he sat behind his desk in the oval office each morning. As a senator, Kennedy did not have access to top-secret military intelligence; consequently, he had been somewhat critical of what he believed was President Eisenhower's soft stand on Cuba. JFK may not have been aware that in early 1960, many months before the presidential election that made him Commander in Chief, Eisenhower and experts at the US Central Intelligence Agency had developed a top-secret military strategy for regime change in Cuba that they hoped would benefit the local Cuban population looking for justice and freedom.

By spring of 1961, without full knowledge of their entire military strategy for Cuba, JFK authorized the Joint Chiefs of Staff to undertake the Cuban regime-change plan, having been assured that the local population would welcome and assist Cuban exile freedom fighters. For five days, from April 15 to April 20 of 1961, a CIA paramilitary brigade undertook a dangerous covert mission to overthrow Communist dictator Fidel Castro in Cuba. Through the lens of history, strategic miscommunication between the newly elected US President and the Joint Chiefs of Staff etched failure into the US Cuban mission. Kennedy was unaware that the JCS had based the success of their military strategy at the Cuban Bay of Pigs on superior US air and naval support. Sensitive to innocent civilians, the new US Commander in Chief was not willing to provide naval and air power, and not because he couldn't. He believed it was wrong to kill innocent civilians. The New Frontier Kennedy policy aimed to transform the image of the United States in the

Western Hemisphere into a benevolent partnership for reform: a true alliance for progress devoid of heavy-booted action.

Without naval and air support, CIA leaders quickly realized that the Cuban invasion was doomed from the start. After only three days of battle, the paramilitary brigade surrendered. JFK courageously took full responsibility for the defeat, which he knew made him look foolish and weak in the eyes of the world. His famous words echo even now: "Victory has many fathers. Defeat is an orphan." Kennedy had repeatedly informed Allen Dulles at the CIA that he would not engage in gunboat diplomacy at the Bay of Pigs. He had sent a trusted military aide to the would-be invaders to inform them that there would not be air and ground help for their endeavor. Unfortunately, they did not believe the messenger. Consequently, Fidel Castro met the invasion head-on and prevailed.

Moderns wonder what JFK's position on war in Vietnam might have been. Of course, we can never really know. It was subsequently reported by 2007 that shortly after the Cuban fiasco, when the Joint Chiefs urged him to respond to the advances of Communist insurgents in Laos by invading the remote Southeast Asian country, Kennedy did not hesitate to rebuff their advice. "John Kennedy was more viscerally antiwar than has been reported"[160]

* * *

Soviet Premier Nikita Khruschev, born into a poor family in Southwest Russia in 1894, was delighted with JFK's US defeat in Cuba. Khruschev's grandfather had been a starving, illiterate serf who served in the Czar's army. His father was a coal miner happy to have work that brought his family a modest income. As a young coal miner himself in 1918, Khruschev had become a Bolshevik looking for a better way of life. Beginning in 1921, he served in the Red Army during the Russian Civil War. Strong and conditioned by poverty to be ruthlessly self-serving, Khruschev participated in Stalin's purges throughout the Soviet Union. By 1937, he was head of the Communist Party in Ukraine. After cruelly purging Ukraine of Communist dissidents, Khruschev selectively rebuilt some of the towns and cities that were destroyed during World War II.

Totally pitiless, cold-blooded, and callous by 1949, Nikita Khruschev was named head of the Communist Party in Moscow. When Josef Stalin died in 1953, his merciless leadership left a severe political vacuum throughout the vast Soviet Union. Within the multilingual USSR, approximately 130 different native languages were spoken among more than 100 distinct nationalities all living within its borders. Although ruthless Khruschev became the Soviet Premier, he was never able to consolidate his political power throughout the ethnically diverse nation. Even though living conditions improved somewhat under his leadership and meaningful investments in space exploration occurred, Soviet military hardliners distrusted heartless Nikita Khruschev. He even had poor relations with neighboring Communist China's leader Mao Zedong, who openly scorned him.

Castro's acclaimed victory in April of 1961 at the Cuban Bay of Pigs was a highly desired prize Nikita Khruschev claimed for himself. Soviet hardliners however, decided to take a wait-and-see posture toward Khruschev as they clamored for increased spending on nuclear weapons of mass destruction. In Washington, DC, intellectually savvy President Kennedy, always a man with a long view of global history, was undeterred by the US international defeat in Cuba. He and his team were even more determined to obtain meaningful concessions from the Soviets regarding nuclear proliferation simply because they were more scientifically advanced about the human and planetary harm such weapons inflict.

The first stop of Kennedy's first foreign trip was Paris where JFK was able to engage in three days of friendly discussions with French President Charles de Gaulle. Jacqueline noted that Madam de Gaulle seemed long-suffering and tired. Rose Kennedy was delighted to accompany her son and daughter-in-law although now in a far less important role than she had once enjoyed. JFK's mother had learned soft diplomacy as a young daughter of Boston's powerful mayor and then as wife of the authoritative US Ambassador to Great Britain immediately preceding World War II.

It was a quiet satisfaction for Rose Kennedy that she was the mother of America's youngest president, but she later admitted that her habit was to pray instinctively and incessantly.[161] Perhaps that discipline was exactly what her son, daughter-in-law, and President and Madam Charles de Gaulle needed at that auspicious historical time. Of course, de Gaulle and his French cohorts were uninformed about the pain-consumed US President who endured such severe back problems, intensified by his long flight to Europe, that he was forced to use crutches in private. For fearless Jack Kennedy, however, pain patiently endured built character and reinforced his resilience, especially in front of his stalwart mother who frequently quoted St. Luke to him: "Of those to whom much has been given much will be required."[162]

On June 4, 1961, John F. Kennedy and Nikita Khruschev finally met face-to-face at the Vienna Summit in Austria. JFK had been informed prior to the meeting that American officials in Berlin were deeply concerned that the Soviets would force Kennedy to pull out of the US shared occupation of Berlin, the German capital that had been negotiated among the four powers at the conclusion of World War II. The mindset of the two world leaders was fundamentally different, though they both represented victorious World War II nations. Khruschev was "the roly-poly leader who, clowning and growling, had at first tried to intimidate the young untested American president—and then, after he [would take] his measure of the man, [he would] settle into a mutually respectful quest with him for world peace."[163] JFK knew his Bay of Pigs disaster had cast an ominous shadow over their first meetings. Khruschev was unimpressed with the outward youth and vigor he saw in the US President and treated him with arrogant disdain at Vienna. The Soviet Premier was overheard referring to President Kennedy as a despicable rich boy disinterested in Cuba who had been raised with a silver spoon in his mouth. Khruschev knew of Joseph Kennedy Senior's outspoken isolationism before World War II, which he wrongfully attributed to the young US President. He was heard to disdainfully say: "like father, like son."

Kennedy's position was strong; he left no doubt in the minds of the Russian entourage that the US would fully protect its interests in Berlin. At the Vienna Summit, no one really knows if it was helpful for Soviet-American relations that JFK's mother and Mrs. Khruschev met and discussed their families at a glittering state dinner at Vienna's Schönbrunn Palace. It was obvious that Rose and Jacqueline's refinement and elegance were a stark contrast to the drab plainness of the Russian women at the glittering banquet. Rose liked Nikita Khruschev's wife, finding her to be pleasant and kindly and treated her with warmth and great gentility. Skilled as Rose was with soft diplomacy, she rather enjoyed the strong, sturdy Soviet First Lady, whom she later defined as "capable of extreme physical exertion." Mrs. Khruschev, a former teacher, spoke a bit of English but showed interest only in Rose's beauty regimen.[164] First Lady Jacqueline Kennedy however, totally charmed Nikita Khruschev, who responded to her kindness with his best manners. Later, when Rose, Jacqueline, and Jack attended Sunday Mass at Vienna's ancient Saint Stephen's Cathedral, fellow worshippers were so enchanted with the dazzling First Family of the United States that they waved white handkerchiefs in their honor.[165] When Rose Kennedy said goodbye to her concerned son before departing for Rome, she reassured him as only a mother can, promising that she would ask for prayers for him and Nikita Khruschev from Pope John XXIII with whom she had a scheduled meeting at the Vatican in the next few days.[166]

JFK quickly reevaluated the Soviet leader's crudeness inherent in his overt disrespect for his US counterparts. Kennedy was not surprised when Khruschev boldly nullified the existing four-party treaty dividing Berlin among the four victors of World War II by boastfully asserting full sovereignty over East

Berlin. A few days later in Washington DC, after he reconsidered the foiled Vienna Summit, Kennedy reported matter-of-factly in a television address to the American people, and indeed to interested world populations, that the Soviet government alone could convert Berlin into a pretext for war. Although the Soviets subsequently built the Berlin Wall, JFK mused that a wall was preferable to a nuclear war. He, however, worked with the Joint Chiefs of Staff and Congress to increase US armed forces to upward of a million soldiers, primarily as a Russian deterrent. Hoping in the long run to redirect the focus of international policy away from war and into space exploration, Kennedy also sought more funding for his envisioned space journeys. Because Congress demanded a balanced budget, defense and space spending impacted the US economy negatively.

The Soviet Premier mistook JFK's strong humanitarian stand against nuclear proliferation as weakness and ordered the resumption of nuclear testing. President Kennedy was aware that the existing bipolar balance of terror between Moscow and the West that he inherited from President Eisenhower rested on Soviet perceptions of US military deterrence. Realpolitik never sleeps. Reluctantly, but realistically, he ordered resumption of US nuclear underground testing. Hardliners in the Soviet Union continued to goad Nikita Khruschev into challenging the West. In US diplomatic circles, none were ever certain whether Soviet hardliners had actual access to nuclear weapons. Battle-tested JFK and his team were constantly confronted head-on with realpolitik: global peace was their goal. Unfortunately, superior military power held the fragile East-West nuclear balance of terror in check. The global arms race continued to escalate.

The intelligent young US President was rightly concerned about the horror nuclear weapons of mass destruction inflict upon innocent populations and their offspring, the global environment, and indeed, the planet itself. Throughout the US, protective underground bunkers were quietly being built by the more scientifically knowledgeable, but to what purpose? After a massive nuclear strike, the very air everyone must breathe remains deadly for thousands of years. In a speech at the United Nations on September 25, 1961, President Kennedy fearlessly called upon every nation to join together to create a world of peace. Though many scoffed, science-trained realists understood.

At Christmas of 1961, JFK and his little family were on holiday at the Kennedy family estate in Palm Beach, Florida. A disturbed man travelled to Palm Beach determined to destroy the young president. He would later claim that when he saw a newspaper photo of JFK with his beautiful wife Jacqueline, tiny Caroline and her younger infant brother, familiarly known then as John-John, perhaps entering Saint Edwards Church for Sunday Mass, he turned away. It had been his intention to self-immolate with explosives that would destroy the US President. When finally captured, he asserted he could not harm a young mother and her babies. The Christmas holiday of 1961 held another shock for the Kennedy family. Seventy-three-year-old Joseph Kennedy Senior suffered a massive stroke that left him impaired for the rest of his life. The much loved and consulted patriarch would now be restrained from active participation in his family's life, but he, like his cherished Rose, would become a man of prayer and sacrifice for them until the end of no end.

His father's stroke brought JFK immediately to Joe Kennedy's bedside where the patriarch lingered between life and death for several days. By tactical political design, few outside his family were aware of Joe's severely compromised health. His father's unexpected stroke was an added incentive for the US President to use whatever time he had left wisely. A man ontologically ahead of his time, well-travelled JFK knew that nuclear disarmament was a global necessity for the survival not only of the planet but of humankind itself. The probability of such humanitarian behavior among the world's elites of the day was unlikely given the aftershocks of World War II, the weakness of human nature, and the mistaken perception that superior nuclear armaments held the key to national survival. JFK and his team's zeal for global peace continuously collided with realpolitik. The Bay of Pigs defeat continued to test respect for Kennedy's presidential leadership to the extreme both at home and abroad.

The ominous dates of October 16 to October 29, 1962, infected the entire world with deathly fear of a nuclear Armageddon. Secret photographs obtained by a US U-2 spy plane over Cuba revealed Soviet construction of high-powered nuclear missiles aimed directly at the United States. The bold audacity of such Russian aggression brought the world's two superpowers to the very brink of global nuclear annihilation.

As JFK studied Cuban missile photos, his goal became very clear. A world leader who never chose fear over faith, Kennedy was determined that somehow, through Kind Providence, he would find a way to protect his own people, Russian civilians, and indeed, the entire population of the earth from the hideous consequences of all-out nuclear war. JFK conferred continuously with military and scientific experts about their informed estimates of US devastation occurring from Soviet nuclear missiles in Cuba that were aimed at the US. The Joint Chiefs of Staff assured their commander in chief that they had at least 27,000 nuclear weapons available and were confident they could obliterate Russia and all its territories with a first strike if Soviet hardliners failed to cooperate. No one among them was exactly certain at that time what the Russian military arsenal actually contained; their Cuban missiles were dangerous beyond doubt and the US military was rightfully determined to eliminate them. But at what cost? The initial nuclear exchange between the US and the Soviets would have been more than a hundred times greater than the Hiroshima bomb. All humankind would be exposed to the deadly nuclear fallout. No one could calculate the massive nuclear effect upon the planet. Some scientists speculated that human life would be impossible on earth, and perhaps never again after a nuclear war.

On October 22, 1962, President Kennedy announced the clear and present global danger for all humankind in a nationally televised address that was carried around the world. He was forthright about the possibility of Soviet-initiated extinction of life on earth. JFK made it quite clear that Soviet offensive weapons of mass destruction aimed at the US could not remain in Cuba under any circumstances. His words were strong, measured, and straightforward; it was unthinkable that a human political power would trigger war resulting in global annihilation. Kennedy declared a US Naval quarantine of all Soviet ships attempting to approach Cuba.

It was now a matter of waiting. Deadly hypotheses awakened slumbering populations of the world and their politicians. Would godless Communist Russian leadership destroy the earth and its people? Would human error trigger nuclear annihilation? Would evil triumph? No one knew if there would be a tomorrow. Many prayed as never before. Churches and places of worship remained opened round the clock. Those with knowledge of the deadly destruction nuclear war would bring felt helpless. JFK was determined to find back channels of opportunity not only for the US dangling on the precipice of eradication, but also for Russian leaders, whoever they were, that would allow the peace to prevail. Few world leaders knew anything about the spiritual integrity of John F. Kennedy. Even fewer trusted brash Soviet Party Chairman Khruschev.[167]

The Monroe Doctrine had been in place since 1823 when President James Monroe defined the role of the United States in the Western Hemisphere. Any European interference in the Western Hemisphere would be viewed as a hostile act. The purpose of American alliances was and is to preserve the independence and safety of nations. It was and remains shocking to this day that tiny Cuba would host nuclear weapons aimed at the United States. Cuban and Soviet leadership unfortunately had misunderstood the Bay of Pigs fiasco. It was certainly a monumental exercise in restraint that allowed the enlightened leadership in the new Kennedy administration to endure such embarrassment on the world stage.

At that time, few recognized that a new kind of leadership was emerging that brought with it respect for human life heretofore unheard of in any nation's foreign policy. Little did it matter that tiny Cuba served as a provocateur backed by a Soviet Goliath attired in nuclear weapons of mass destruction. Simple moral clarity identified in the New Testament inaugurated a new time in world history where people of goodwill simply did unto others as they would have done to themselves. But now, the reward they wanted for their noble acts was simple human survival.

History is clear that the nuclear Armageddon in October of 1962 rightfully frightened a war-weary world peopled with many who did know who their provocateur really was.[168] JFK may have personally discerned that the United States was facing rogue principalities and powers gleefully calling forth the Armageddon furies. Ever a tested man of destiny, John F. Kennedy could rely on the inexplicable power of Kind Providence to guide his way. His calm demeanor perhaps belied his own interior concerns. There is much about this American President that we will never know. There is no personal record of those momentous days when nuclear Armageddon hung like a sword of Damocles over all United States leadership.[169]

Like most knowledgeable people in the United States, President Kennedy knew the unthinkable consequences of a nuclear first strike. Retaliation was the only option. Global death would result. Reluctantly, Jack Kennedy acquiesced to his wife's request that his tiny family should face death together. The President arranged for Jacqueline and their two tiny children to return to the White House to await their fate together. All over the world, other families aware of the clear and present danger of nuclear annihilation were similarly huddled together awaiting Armageddon.

PART III

Freedom's Triumph

*Speaking for the United States of America . . .
we believe that truth is stronger than error—
and that freedom is more enduring than coercion.
And in the contest for a better life,
all the world can be a winner.*
—John F. Kennedy

SEVEN

Cuban Missile Crisis

*We shall do our part to build a world of peace
where the weak are safe and the strong are just . . .
Confident and unafraid, we labor on—
not toward a strategy of annihilation
but toward a strategy of peace.*
—John F. Kennedy

The hand of fate manifests in inexplicable ways that humankind too often overlooks. There is always an overriding wind of Divine Providence guiding, soothing, directing poor, unconscious humans to heights unimaginable. The calming hand of fate gently assures there is a time for everything under the Heavens. JFK believed: "The great revolution in the history of man, past, present and future, is the revolution of those determined to be free."[170]

As early as 1950, Joseph P. Kennedy, Senior had been observing to anyone who would listen to him that the policies coming out of Washington should focus on protecting freedom-loving Americans from godless Communist infiltration. His second son, then Senator Kennedy was disturbed by the Eisenhower policy of spending vast sums in difficult areas of the emerging world, especially in the Far East, yet had almost a blind eye for the poverty and needs of developing states in the American Hemisphere. Senator John Kennedy, always a purple heart combat veteran at heart, respected Eisenhower's belief that a strong military is the best defense against aggression. His first best-selling book *Why England Slept* had laid out his personal observations about laissez-faire governments that sleep through their surrounding enemies expensive military buildups. While his father served as US Ambassador in London, Harvard student JFK had met the British Prime Minister Neville Chamberlain who mistakenly thought he had brokered a peace deal with Hitler. Unfortunately, Chamberlain had not recognized that the stronger a nation's military, the more likely that government will succeed in negotiations with potential enemies. Consequently, a half million British military perished in World War II perhaps because of its laissez-faire governmental political views preceding the Second World War.

President John F. Kennedy was aware that nuclear bombs dropped on Hiroshima and Nagasaki changed international diplomacy forever although few were so aware at that time. The East-West confrontation that resulted from the final settlement of World War II at Yalta left the Soviet block of nations with nuclear weapons of mass destruction intended for its first strike foreign policy. The United States was led by President Harry Truman, who was followed by President Dwight D. Eisenhower from 1952 until 1960 when John F. Kennedy assumed the reigns of the young United States Presidency. Eisenhower, a West Point graduate, was the five-star general who organized the significant military campaigns of World War II. These included Operation Torch in North Africa in 1942-43, the invasion of Normandy in 1944, and the Battle of the Bulge. Eisenhower succeeded as Supreme Allied Commander in Western Europe and at World War II's conclusion united the member-nations of NATO. Ike was globally recognized as a splendid theoretician who understood the destructive power of war.

JFK's approach to foreign policy was no less realistic and pragmatic. He had observed the strategies of the Eisenhower era from his senate seat and acknowledged the skill and wisdom of Secretary of State John Foster Dulles and his brother Allen Dulles who headed the CIA during the 1950s. Kennedy recognized however, that many in Washington, especially those who remained loyal to Eisenhower's vice president, Richard Nixon, were disturbed by Kennedy's victory.

Both Kennedy and Khruschev faced the 1962 Cuban Missile Crisis with knowledge of prophetic celestial warnings flowing from Fatima, Portugal in 1917 concerning Earth and its population. After extensive investigation, the Vatican had formally ratified the authenticity of the Fatima celestial warnings in 1930. Two of three Fatima prophetic geopolitical warnings became widely known. These included the possibility of avoiding World War II. If World War II did occur, the aftermath would include Russia spreading terrors based on errors throughout the world, which could culminate in a vision so terrible it was deemed to be hell on earth: an inferno of inescapable poisonous air everywhere occasioned by raging impact fire that licks and spits and tosses screaming humans high into the sky before gulping each one down into its vast hellhole; human suffering so unbearable that the living envy the dead.[171] Senator Kennedy was personally interviewed on TV by Fatima expert John Haffert during his presidential campaign. Haffert had focused the interview on the Fatima geopolitical celestial warnings.

By 1960, global geopolitical intrigue led Vatican-trained diplomat Pope John XXIII to conclude decisively that public release of an expected third Fatima warning would be imprudent. Instead, he shocked his peers by planning and convening the Second Vatican Council shortly before the Cuban Missile Crisis became publicly known. Although his Fatima decision of 1960 remains controversial, and few comprehend the magnitude of the Third Fatima warning issued in the year 2000, Pope Saint John XXIII made certain that clergy of the Russian Orthodox hierarchy were present at the Vatican for his Second Ecumenical Council. He strategized that their presence would guarantee the highest echelons of leadership within the USSR would have full knowledge of Council teachings as the Cuban missile crisis unfolded globally.

In the mid-twentieth century, Spanish artist Salvador Dali was one of the richest, most famous painters in the world. His art was on display in most of the world's significant museums and galleries. Lithographs and prints of the Spanish painter's unique work were available to most households in North America. It was well known that Dali had long ago abandoned his Catholic faith. John Haffert, on behalf of the twenty-five-million-member Blue Army of Fatima that he co-founded, arranged for Mr. Dali to personally interview the last remaining visionary of Fatima, Sister Lucia, by now a middle aged, Carmelite nun residing in a cloistered convent in Coimbra, Portugal. Lucia was widely known to say that even in the worst of us, there remains a spark of goodness. It was hoped that Sister Lucia could explain to Salvador Dali what she and the other two tiny children visionaries saw when the earth opened up and revealed "hell" where poor sinners go who have no one to pray and do penance for them. Haffert hoped that one painting by the famous artist would be worth a thousand words.

Godlessness had become popular in the 1960s; a comfortable, guilt-free way of life within elite, totalitarian-centered Communism, and even among those worldwide who refused to trouble themselves about the welfare of their neighbors. Drugs and heavy alcohol consumption flowed freely throughout the war-weary world. The luxurious American residence of Salvador Dali was the elite St. Regis Hotel in New York City. It was there, on behalf of the entire Blue Army of Fatima, that John Haffert convinced Salvatore Dali to interview cloistered Sister Lucia. Haffert commissioned Salvatore Dali to create a canvas depicting the vision of hell that the tiny Fatima children seers saw. Dali, who had considered himself a convenient atheist, subsequently spent time with Sister Lucia at her convent in Coimbra, Portugal. As many would learn through him, words spoken and received without the help of the Holy Spirit, convey little. Afterward, the world-famous artist did his best to paint his meager understanding of the visionary's eye-witness vision of hell as he understood her through translators. Only many years later, at the twilight of his life, did Salvatore Dali personally undergo what he then understood was his personal experience of man-made hell on earth.

Five years before his death, Dali was confined to a sickbed. Suddenly, electrical sparks from his handheld buzzer ignited Dali's bedclothes with fire. Quickly his sickroom filled with blinding smoke as the consuming electrical fire leapt to nearby curtains and carpets. The skin on Dali's right leg was devoured by the raging fires as he rolled to the floor from his burning bed and struggled to crawl to an exit. Salvatore Dali's worst ordeal was awareness that he was living in his own Fatima hell. He escaped hell's fire as a changed man.[172] Though Dali never recovered from his fire-filled rendezvous with death, he reembraced the faith of his youth with joy and fulfillment. Dali believed that humankind, not God, creates hell on earth. He spoke often about God's will for humans, which is goodness and kindness all the days of our lives now and forever.[173]

Geopolitical intrigue was common in the capitols of the world in Autumn of 1962. The wealthy had untested bomb shelters in their homes designed to protect them from weapons of mass destruction they hoped they would never experience. Everyone seemed to fear that a nuclear war triggered by Washington or Moscow threatened them. Even young school children were taught to evacuate their classrooms and seek refuge in designated shelters. Few then could comprehend that nuclear holocaust is indeed man-made hell on earth. Those unfortunates who are still alive after a nuclear blast certainly envy the dead.

Diplomat Pope John XXIII was convivial, prayerful, perhaps even a mystic. He respected and enjoyed people of all backgrounds. While on assignment in Turkey during World War II, he had happily prayed his rosary on beads any passerby could easily see as he walked daily in the public square. Having spent most of his ecclesial life in diplomatic service, he was keenly aware of the global perils inherent in nuclear proliferation. As Pope, John strove to re-energize not only the ancient Catholic Church, but also the spiritual consciences of all people with the magnificent truths revealed in the person of Jesus Christ, Incarnate Son of God. His goal for the Second Vatican Council was to help everyone throughout the world rediscover humanity's true dignity and purpose. [174]

The aim was magnificent. Twenty-seven hundred high-ranking prelates attended the Second Vatican Council. Also in attendance were delegates representing most Protestant denominations, along with dignitaries from the Eastern Orthodox Church of the Middle East and, significantly, of the Russian Orthodox Church. The prejudices of the ages were less of a hindrance than an intellectual stumbling block. At best, hidden pride guiding unaware leaders playing to their constituents led to confusion that too often emerged in innocent journalistic interpretations of Council documents.

Pope John greatly desired that the Second Vatican Council would rekindle the evangelical fire of Christocentric faith that had animated the Apostles. Indeed, the Second Vatican Council sought to find expression for ancient, enduring truths in modern language and linguistic presentation. Pope John envisioned a Council that would provide a new Pentecost: awareness of the unconditional love of God for every human breaking into time and space that would console and enliven all the fragmented, war-weary populations of the world. The ways of the Almighty, however, are rarely visible immediately.

THE SPIRITUAL LEGACY OF JOHN F. KENNEDY

In the early 1960s, people throughout the world were consciously less traumatized by memories of the atrocities of World War. The arts thrived; magazines and Hollywood fed the hedonistic dreams and longings of the war-weary public. Prosperity seemed available for anyone who worked hard. Subtle immorality, however, quietly escalated in the glitter of quasi-atheism as instant gratification laced with personal pleasure became a sought-after reality. A vision of hell, or thoughts of another global war, or nuclear annihilation were at best, unwelcome in 1962.

Geopolitics never sleep. Eleven days after the opening of the Second Ecumenical Council, on October 22, 1962, American Catholic President John F. Kennedy announced that US spy planes had discovered Soviet missile bases in Cuba. Nuclear experts determined that the Soviet medium-range missiles on the Island of Cuba, only ninety miles from Key West, Florida, were capable of direct nuclear hits on populous cities in the US, including New York, Boston, and Washington, DC. There is little doubt that Russian leader Nikita Khrushchev, perhaps not as well informed as JFK about the inherent horror of nuclear Armageddon, had access to the prophetic geopolitical celestial warnings of Fatima through clandestine channels within the KGB.

Pragmatic Jack Kennedy had no compunction about seeking backdoor options from world leaders as he and his team strategized ways to avert global nuclear annihilation. He reached out to Norman Cousins, editor of *Saturday Review*, whom he knew had contacts both in Russia and inside the Vatican. Cousins was working with Soviet writers and scientists in Andover,

Massachusetts at the time and had previously acknowledged that in the bipolar world of nuclear brinkmanship, the papacy was the only third force.[175] Cousins, a true American patriot, was able to get a message to Pope John asking for any and all help he would undertake to persuade Khruschev to back off from pushing the US over the brink into nuclear first strike mode. It is widely believed that Pope John responded with two statements that helped procure the peace. On October 24, 1962, during his weekly radio address, Pope John urged both the Soviet Union and the US to show restraint saying: "*The Pope always speaks well of those statesmen, on whatever side, who strive to come together to avoid war and bring peace to humanity.*" Shortly thereafter, the Pope sent a private message to the Soviet Embassy in Rome stating, "*To promote, encourage, and accept negotiations, always and on every level, is a rule of wisdom that draws down heavenly and earthly blessings.*"[176]

United States policy experts recognize that through Norman Cousins's patriotic efforts, John F. Kennedy unobtrusively but effectively offered Nikita Khruschev an opportunity to save face, stand down, and hold himself out globally as a distinguished statesman, a man of peace. Such nobility for whatever reason always eclipses devastating confrontation. It is not known exactly how effective the good offices of Pope John XXIII were at the time with hardliners in the USSR, or even if it his efforts were as effective as stated. As long as the world exists, however, history acknowledges Pope John's diplomatic pathway to peace.[177] Meanwhile, having engaged in creative, nondisclosed backchannels from the White House, including diplomatic and consular contacts at home and abroad, the US President assigned his trusted brother Robert F. Kennedy, Attorney General of the United States to negotiate a top-secret peace settlement with the Soviets through the Russian Ambassador in Washington, DC. As a result, President Kennedy's naval blockade of Russian ships heading to Cuba proved effective.[178] Both Moscow and Washington chose peace rather than global nuclear annihilation. Nikita Khruschev later admitted that he developed a deep respect for Kennedy during the crisis. He admired that JFK didn't let himself become frightened nor did he become reckless. Khruschev believed Kennedy showed wisdom and statesmanship when he turned his back on right-wing forces in the United States who may have been trying to goad him into taking first-strike military action.[179]

Pope John was widely quoted at the time when he said on Vatican Radio: *"I beg heads of state not to remain insensitive to the cry of humanity, peace, peace. Let them do all that is in their power to save peace; in this way they will avoid the horrors of war, the appalling consequences of which no one could predict. Let them continue to negotiate. History will see this loyal and open attitude as a witness to conscience. To promote, encourage, and accept negotiations, always and on every level, is a rule of wisdom that draws down both heavenly and earthly blessings."*

Notwithstanding Soviet hard-liners' staunch never yield an inch attitudes, Nikita Khrushchev experienced the mysterious hand of fate. He chose life when many around him ignorantly clamored for death. Wisdom inexplicably showed Khruschev that he held the terrifying power to make the earth a wasteland where no possibility of life can exist. The shock of such human arrogance astounded the Soviet leader. No one really knows how Khruschev experienced his personal rendezvous with truth. He later wrote in his memoirs "*Any fool can start a war, and once he's done so, even the wisest of men are helpless to stop it—especially if it's a nuclear war.*"[180] Nikita Khruschev chose to close the Cuban missile bases and ordered all Soviet ships to return to Russia.

It requires little imagination to see the vision of hell experienced by the tiny children seers of Fatima on July 13, 1917, as a preview of suffering endured by global victims of an all-out nuclear attack. Moreover, nuclear war could alter humankind's genetic structure and cause a deformed environment.[181] People who knew Pope John XXIII reasonably well said that he rightfully believed Christianity exists to serve the planet and its people.[182] Shepherding Fatima's celestial warnings, he announced publicly: "*The Russian people are a wonderful people. We must not condemn them because we do not like their political system. They have a deep spiritual inheritance which they have not lost. We can talk with them. We must always try to speak to the goodness that is in people. Nothing is lost in the attempt. Everything may be lost if men do not find a way to work together to save peace.*"[183]

Like US President John F. Kennedy, the atheistic Soviet Premier Nikita Khruschev became an anonymous agent of Kind Providence as the two leaders guided their nations toward a peaceful exit from the Cuban Missile Crisis. People of character understand there is a price to be paid for real statesmanship. Khruschev endured his military advisors' scorn as some blatantly accused him of being a traitor to the Fatherland. Honest history, however, recognizes that the US and Soviet leaders preserved the national honor of their nations as they protected contemporary humankind and the planet and preserved both for subsequent generations.

Although global leaders remain concerned about nuclear Armageddon, Pope John and his successors have been deeply troubled about the immortal souls of the global population as well as of the earth's environment. The consequences to everyone if global conversion should fail are catastrophic. On December 26, 1962, aged Pope John XXIII knelt on the floor of his bedroom before a crucifix and consecrated the final sacrifice of his life for the conversion of all Russia to harmony with Christians in the West. He believed that with such accord the world could taste lasting peace.

Experts continue to refer to World War II, which lasted from 1939 to 1945 as the deadliest military conflict in history. More than 75 million people died during that war. The Soviet Union suffered the highest casualties with upwards of 25 million deaths. Of that number, 19 million Soviets were civilians. Starvation, homelessness, separation of families including young children, horrendous crimes against humanity, gulags, concentration camps, battles, and bombings in urban areas, along with destruction of property rights, and political and economic systems, caused human misery that belongs in the lowest rungs of Dante's Inferno.

Although John F. Kennedy and Nikita Khruschev chose paths of peace in late October of 1962, geopolitical crises continue to plague decisionmakers worldwide. Humanity holds vast power for good or evil, life or death. It is little wonder that the hand of fate, the hidden presence of God in the history of humankind, allowed Khruschev to be deeply touched by JFK's inaugural address on January 20, 1961, and had it published in Pravda for all the literate in the USSR to ponder. Little imagination is necessary to realize that the vision of hell the tiny children visionaries of Fatima saw at Fatima on July 13, 1917, was in fact, a vision of those suffering from the effects of a nuclear Armageddon. Those not fortunate enough to die immediately on impact are in effect victims of inescapable nuclear fire which is hell on earth. Survivors most certainly envy the dead as they strangulate on highly toxic nuclear fumes that render the earth uninhabitable for thousands of years, if ever.

Highly trained diplomats are aware of significant pulsations of spirituality among the vast populations of the earth. They are also aware that misguided people tend to feed on one another. Prophetic celestial geopolitical warnings at Fatima, inexplicable cures at Lourdes, and miracles at Mexico City attributed to Our Lady of Guadalupe transcend culture and nationality for they are universal human treasure that belongs to no one person or place. Modern, well-trained world leaders know of Fatima's celestial geopolitical warnings and hopefully do their best to avert nuclear Armageddon. Fortunately, no one of good conscience is ignorant enough to succumb to parochial superstition. Through the deep lens of history, an American historian recognized the subtle hand of fate contained in the elusive innuendo within JFK's inaugural address: "Kennedy did not want Moscow to see his administration as intent on an apocalyptic showdown between East and West. To the contrary . . . his speech was an invitation to find common ground against a devastating nuclear war."[184] And so they did.

In his memoirs, Nikita Khruschev wrote of his nefarious understanding of other tools of mass destruction: "There are other weapons too which are necessary to have in any eventuality, namely chemical and bacteriological weapons."[185] Those who survived the global pandemic of 2020 ponder the inherent dangers of geopolitical malaise among nations. Wisdom hints that enemies of the United States learn through Khruschev's own words: "Any fool can start a war, and once he's done so, even the wisest of man are helpless to stop it—especially if it's a nuclear war."[186] The same can be said for bioterrorism devolving into an uncontrollable global pandemic.

EIGHT

The Invisible Hand of Fate

*Let us see if we, in our own time,
can move the world
to a just and lasting peace.*[187]
—John F. Kennedy

In the final year of his life, JFK tackled head-on three of the gravest problems that continue to confront knowledgeable humankind worldwide: nuclear devastation, poverty, and bigotry.

Kennedy had promises to keep but only a few more miles to go. He vigorously encouraged federally supported housing legislation that improved living conditions for many who languished in poverty, especially African Americans. To the delight of civil rights activists, JFK pushed the Area Redevelopment Act through Congress which allocated federal funds to poverty-stricken states. Overt and covert Ku Klux Klansmen along with other bigots, however, remained vigilant in blocking integration in public transportation and education.[188] Such fundamental human injustice often erupted in violence, particularly in the southern states where racism was virulent. Patriotic people, especially those serving in the Kennedy administration who wanted to shine light on this grave social injustice, encouraged colleagues, associates, and friends to resign from nonintegrated clubs and avoid segregated hotels and restaurants. Undoubtedly, they were aware that they were offering a band-aid for a gaping wound, but they were determined to help even if only in such small ways. In spite of massive civil rights difficulties, JFK remained popular among black voters. Any and all possible civil rights improvements were a high priority for John F. Kennedy.

Early American Pilgrims hoped that the US might one day become the breadbasket of the world. Those close to New Englander Jack Kennedy quickly realized that although he was highly interested in finding ways to eliminate global hunger, he was indeed laser focused on poverty, especially in inner cities at home. A leader ahead of his time, he was committed to federally funded health care for the elderly, and federal aid for excellent education that he hoped would eventually spread to all cultures everywhere. Jack Kennedy and his beautiful, cultured wife Jacqueline became renowned for the glittering state dinners they hosted at the White House at which the healthiest foods available were consistently served. Although President Kennedy had other things on his mind than social events, he dutifully attended White House galas even though his severe back pain, coupled with Addison's disease and probable Celiac's disease made such long evenings a difficult challenge. The Kennedy guest lists were always comprised of racially and politically diverse notables that included artists, Hollywood stars, musicians, academics, scientists, clergy, military and business leaders. Often, Jack Kennedy found inspiration from other intelligent leaders, and he listened carefully to their insights and suggestions. His manners were impeccable. His charm rarely wavered.

John F. Kennedy was a disciplined, compassionate leader with high respect for commitments honored. James Meridith, a black Air Force veteran who served in the US military from 1951-1960, attempted to begin classes at the University of Mississippi in autumn of 1962. The Mississippi governor, Ross Barnett, was loath to accept the university's federally mandated integration policy and did his best to block Meridith's entrance. Federal marshals were on hand to ensure that Meridith remained safe amidst an unpeaceful, protesting mob. Foolish voices were heard to call for Meredith's lynching. Notwithstanding the exploding riots, Governor Barnett ordered the withdrawal of all state troopers. The few federal marshals on duty were unable to contain the university mob, which quickly devolved into a terror cell bent on destruction of life and property. A young British student and a French journalist were murdered. More than 200 others were injured. Only after US Attorney General Robert Kennedy, with the full support of President Kennedy and his entire administration, provided additional federal troops to clear the campus was peace restored. James Meridith, continuously guarded by federal troops, successfully matriculated at the University of Mississippi.[189]

In a televised address from Washington DC on September 30, 1962, President Kennedy stated: "... Mr. James Meridith is now in residence on the campus of the University of Mississippi ... this is at it should be for our nation is founded on the principle that observance of the law is the eternal safeguard of liberty and defiance of the law is the surest road to tyranny. The law which we must obey includes the final rulings of the courts, as well as the enactments of our legislative bodies. Even among law-abiding men few laws are universally loved, but they are uniformly respected and not resisted. Americans are free, in short, to disagree with the law but not to disobey it. For in a government of laws and not of men, no man, however prominent or powerful, and no mob, however unruly or boisterous, is entitled to defy a court of law. If this country should ever reach the point where any man or group of men by force or threat of force could long defy the commands of our Court and our Constitution, then no law would stand free from doubt, no judge would be sure of his writ, and no citizen would be safe from his neighbors . . . Let us preserve both the law and the peace, and then, healing those wounds that are within we can turn to the greater crises that are without and stand united as one people in our pledge to man's freedom."[190]

The President and his team were deeply saddened in early summer of 1963, when Medgar Evers, local leader of the National Association for the Advancement of Colored People was shot in the back by an angry bigot as he got out of his car at his home in Jackson, Mississippi. Forty US cities succumbed to riots protesting the assassination of the Mississippi NAACP leader.

On May 11, 1963, when a bomb exploded near the hotel where Reverend Doctor Martin Luther King Jr. was staying, mob violence erupted again in the streets of Birmingham. Protest riots broke out in inner cities throughout the US. Most Americans, including the black population, had respect for law and order and peace was restored. Managing mob violence was no easy process. Although JFK knew that bold civil rights legislation was necessary, Congress had no appetite for it. The Kennedy administration instructed federal administrators and federal workers to boycott businesses where racial discrimination was customary. Although racial integration decisions flowed continuously from the courts, bigotry lingered. JFK had consistently appealed personally to business, community, and religious leaders for peaceful integration. His dream was enlightened humanity as envisioned by the Founders of the US.

* * *

On June 9, 1963, Kennedy spoke at American University in Washington DC. He reiterated his science-based knowledge that only worldwide nuclear disarmament could save the planet and its inhabitants. President Kennedy's remarks that day live on in the aspirations of patriots everywhere and are included in Appendix Four. War-scarred European powers were opposed to disarmament, especially leaders in the United Kingdom. France was fast becoming a formidable nuclear power and Germany, with its Berlin Wall separating Communist East Berlin from Democratic West Berlin was not sympathetic to nuclear disarmament. Paradoxically, nuclear warheads were becoming a self-preservation way of life steeped in global death. Many, without science-based knowledge, believed in the old ways of war: "Get them before they get us." In an all-out nuclear war, everyone dies, some more quickly than others. Ongoing nuclear WMD testing, however, is a slow death of the earth and its people.

On June 26, 1963, US President John F. Kennedy stood as an icon of peace in West Berlin at the famous Berlin Wall. More than half a million people gathered to hear him speak for all freedom-loving individuals of all times and places as he cried out to past, present, and future generations "Ich bib ein Berliner" (I am a Berliner). JFK's haunting words of solidarity with all justice-seekers became a beacon of hope shining brilliantly at the front line of the Cold War. Idealistic US national harmony had inspired Kennedy in the South Pacific during World War II. At the Berlin Wall, the multitudes saw a tested leader who would gladly give his one life to help bring peace among broken, tired freedom-seekers of fundamental justice throughout the world.

A month later, Kennedy addressed the nation, and the world in a televised speech from the presidential oval office. In clear language, JFK explained the urgent necessity of a nuclear test ban treaty, even though few trusted its enforceability. By now, the US President was viewed internationally as a man of peace. Nuclear proliferation escalated as India, Pakistan, and Israel developed their own nuclear arsenals. Clandestine nuclear testing of WMDs then as now impacts the global environment in ways humankind may never fully understand. In JFK's era, however, few, if any, nuclear experts were even somewhat aware of the severe long-term environmental harm nuclear WMD testing inflicts on the planet and its inhabitants. Deep distrust of the Soviet Union weighed heavily upon US foreign policymakers. Most remained heavily scarred by the nuclear holocaust the world narrowly escaped during the Soviet-triggered Cuban Missile Crisis.

It is said that President Kennedy, the evening of his speech at the Berlin Wall, began to make notes for a speech that would never be spoken by him personally, although its written power would become immortalized. "I pledged in 1960 that a new administration would strive to secure for every American his full constitutional rights . . ."[191]

A year after the Second Vatican Council opened its ecumenical door to all people everywhere and the Cuban missile crisis that ignited terror throughout the world was ameliorated, Baptist Reverend Dr. Martin Luther King, Jr. led protesting marchers through the streets of Birmingham, Alabama pleading for racial justice. In early May of 1963, Dr. King called for black children to join his march for civil rights. Hundreds were arrested, filling the prisons of Birmingham to capacity. For unknown reasons, a local police captain is said to have ordered high-powered water jets to be unleashed upon the peaceful young protesters. Far away in Washington, DC, civil rights experts attempted to negotiate a peaceful solution for black leaders. They failed.

Racial tension continued to influence US domestic policy. Interracial sibling unity inched along with little fanfare when James Meridith earned a bachelor's degree at the University of Mississippi in August of 1963. Civil rights leaders, however, called for a march on Washington, DC. Upwards of 250,000 justice seekers gathered at the Lincoln Memorial on a sweltering, late summer afternoon demanding federal jobs, fair wages, and economic, educational, and voting fairness. Leaders pleaded for civil rights protections guaranteeing equal justice for all Americans of every race, creed, ethnicity, and nationality.

Poignant words now carved into immortality flowed from his "I Have a Dream" remarks that Reverend Doctor Martin Luther King, Jr. delivered extemporaneously. He slowly ascended the steps of the Lincoln Memorial to deliver dazzling hope to hot, thirsty, needy, and overwrought justice seekers assembled not only before him on that blistering Washington day, but symbolically to all humankind craving freedom.

President Kennedy, deeply touched by the voices of the people that hot August day in late summer, 1963, issued a Presidential statement in response:

"We have witnessed today in Washington tens of thousands of Americans—both Negro and white—exercising their right to assemble peaceably and direct the widest possible attention to a great national issue . . . to secure equal treatment and equal opportunity for all without regard to race, color, creed, or nationality.

Although this summer has seen remarkable progress in translating civil rights from principles into practices, we have a very long way yet to travel. One cannot help but be impressed with the deep fever and the quiet dignity that characterize the thousands who have gathered in the nation's capital from across the country to demonstrate their faith and confidence in our democratic form of government. History has seen many demonstrations of widely varying character and for a whole host of reasons . . . this nation can properly be proud of the demonstration that has occurred here today. The leaders of the organizations sponsoring the march and all who have participated in it deserve our appreciation of the detailed preparations that made it possible and for the orderly manner in which it has been conducted.

The executive branch of the federal government will continue its efforts to obtain increased employment and to eliminate discrimination in employment practices, two of the prime goals of the march. In addition, our efforts to secure enactment of the legislative proposals made to the Congress will be maintained.

The cause of twenty million Negroes has been advanced by the program conducted so appropriately before the shrine to the Great Emancipator, but even more significant is the contribution to all mankind."

As with all great causes, some American journalists questioned the US President on September 12, 1963, whether Kennedy was moving ahead too rapidly on racial justice. JFK replied:

> "... I think you must make a judgment about the movement of a great historical event which is taking place in this country... I think we will stand..."

President John F. Kennedy had prepared a speech for delivery in Austin, Texas on November 22, 1963, in which he intended to say that his administration had: "... opened more new doors to members of minority groups—doors to transportation, voting, education, employment, and places of public accommodation—than had been opened in any three-year or thirty-year period in this century. There is no uncontroversial way to fulfill our constitutional pledge to establish justice and promote domestic tranquility for all, but we intend to fulfill those obligations because they are right."[192]

* * *

In mid-1963, the US Joint Chiefs of Staff advised their commander in chief of their concern about the spread of godless Communism in and around Southeast Asia, especially within the corrupt regime of Ngo Dinh Diem in South Vietnam.

It was widely understood that Diem epitomized what has now been identified as "cafeteria Christianity." Such renegades are little interested in their Christian faith, or their inherent personal responsibility to live their beliefs with actions, not just words. Instead, "cafeteria Christians" simply pick and choose, cafeteria-style, moment by moment expediency—fulfillment of their immediate desires regardless of consequences to others. Unfortunately, cafeteria politics is laced with the same poison. Diem's devout wife had travelled unofficially to Washington, DC seeking help for her weak husband and struggling country. The author learned of an ominous prophesy Madam Diem brought to Washington that allegedly reached the highest levels of the US government in the early days of the Kennedy administration. Pentagon officials believed that without US support, the godless, Communist backed National Liberation Front, the Viet Kong would overthrow presumed highly corrupt, nepotistic Ngo Dinh Diem, whose purportedly unscrupulous brother ruled him and South Vietnam in his stead.

In 1954, when the Vietnamese people cast out their French colonial rulers, the country was divided into North and South Vietnam. Long, cruel civil war ensued. Ho Chi Minh in the north enjoyed generous Soviet and Chinese Communist military support. In exchange, he ruthlessly installed Communist structures to manage North Vietnam's vast, underdeveloped population. President Eisenhower's foreign policy of containment of atheistic Communism in 1954 included US support for South Vietnam that propped up feckless Diem who ruled from Saigon. Early in 1961, the newly inaugurated US President John F. Kennedy had made it clear that on his watch, the independence of emerging nations, including Vietnam, would flow from their own people and not from foreign overlords. Although JFK continued the Eisenhower containment policy in Southeast Asia, his foreign policy did not include internal management within the region. There would be no US interference or additional US troops in Vietnam. Notwithstanding JFK's official policy for South Vietnam, however, the largely invisible wheels of fate occasionally grind forward in unexpected ways. The press of the day, always prowling for human interest stories that attracted readers, would prove a mighty challenge for JFK. Although the reading public gobbled captivating stories of the young First Family living in the White House, few journalists understood at the time that Kennedy's New Frontier aimed to preserve peace worldwide.

As seasonal flooding occurred in South Vietnam's Mekong Delta, and under the guise of humanitarian help, the US Joint Chiefs planned to put combat troops in the region. Their long-term military strategy aimed at blocking the spread of Russian and Chinese backed Communism throughout Southeast Asia. Kennedy denied their request. He believed that the democratic way of life was so superior to repressive, atheistic Communism that eventually emerging populations would disavow leaders who denied their inherent liberty. War hero that he was, JFK was determined to avoid combat in the region. Kennedy was determined that there would be no US war provocation in Southeast Asia or anywhere else on his watch.[193]

Emerging nations learn that the journey toward liberty is often painful along the way. The international press blamed JFK and his policies for allowing corrupt Diem to grab US humanitarian funds for his personal enjoyment while South Vietnamese people starved. President Kennedy was duly informed that civil unrest was a fact of life as Diem's administration became even more oppressive. The population of South Vietnam at that time was largely Buddhist. Diem's ineffectual government clamped down hard on his people, imprisoning their Buddhist leaders and closing their places of worship. By June of 1963, before press cameras of the world, a Buddhist monk self-immolated in Saigon as a protest against the harsh, irresponsible Diem regime. Consequently, diplomatic circles buzzed with activity in Washington. Word quickly reached Diem that he must correct the Buddhist problem immediately and clean up nepotistic corruption in his regime or all US support would end. Henry Cabot Lodge of Massachusetts was named US ambassador to Vietnam with firm instructions to restore peace in the region.

NINE

The Hand of Fate Strikes

*We . . . are by destiny rather than choice—
the watchmen on the walls of world freedom.
We ask, therefore,
that we may be worthy of our power and responsibility,
that we may exercise our strength with wisdom and restraint,
and that we may achieve in our time and for all time,
the ancient vision of 'peace on earth, goodwill toward man.*[194]
—John F. Kennedy

Nothing happens on earth that Divine Providence does not allow. No human penetrates its unfathomable mysteries, but some recognize the ways of Divine Providence. JFK learned that faith is often a choice in the dark night of pain and suffering that he experienced from earliest childhood. He discovered as a young teenager to trust Mother Mary's intercession on his behalf. He believed that Christ's wisdom shines through her to her faith-filled children, especially those close to her in good times and bad times, too.[195] Jack Kennedy, like his immigrant ancestors, guarded the faith given to him from the cradle. He silently acquired refined trust in Divine Providence, also known secularly as the "hand of fate", rooted in his personal experiences of hardship, especially during World War II in the bloody Pacific.

In early August of 1963, the US President did his utmost to clear his desk in the oval office so that he could join his young family summering at Cape Cod. First Lady Jacqueline Kennedy, along with her two very young presidential children, awaited the birth of their fifth child at the family's summer home in Hyannis Port, Massachusetts. Every precaution available to obstetric medical science at the time was available to the beautiful, beloved wife of the President of the United States.

August 7, 1963, marked the twentieth anniversary of the providential rescue of John F. Kennedy in the Solomon Islands during World War II. Both the First Lady and the President celebrated JFK's highly unlikely rescue in different ways. Although in her third trimester of pregnancy, Mrs. Kennedy accompanied her two little children to nearby Osterville so that they could enjoy a pony ride. Unexpected labor pains surprised the First Lady, and she was rushed by helicopter to medical facilities at nearby Otis Air Force Base. Her six weeks premature son, weighing little more than four pounds, was born by emergency caesarian surgery at Otis while the struggling infant's father was enroute on Air Force One.

When the US President arrived, he quickly sent for the hospital chaplain who immediately baptized the presidential second son whom Jack and Jacqueline named Patrick Bouvier Kennedy. Aware of the infant's severe breathing difficulties, JFK disregarded standard hospital protocol and personally wheeled his second son's incubator to the bedside of his cherished wife. Their prayers of hope for their suffering second son were so intense that Jacqueline collapsed in inexplicable grief. Stalwart

THE HAND OF FATE STRIKES

JFK, who had faced down death on four previous occasions, humbly comforted his wife as best he could as he increased his own prayers for her and their besieged newborn son. A pediatric specialist from Boston Children's Hospital was flown by helicopter to Otis Air Force Base where he diagnosed tiny Patrick's respiratory distress and recommended the infant's immediate transfer to Boston Children's Hospital where the most advanced neonatal treatment in the world was available. President Kennedy did not leave his struggling newborn second son during his thirty-nine hours of life on earth. A harrowing ambulance ride to Boston Children's Hospital was followed by Herculean medical efforts to save the presidential infant. Hospital observers were amazed at the love, strength, and passion JFK exhibited as he stood watch by his suffering second son's incubator. He and Jacqueline wept publicly when their darling infant died. His raw courage and her prayerful love blended in poignancy only the blessed perceive.

Some suggested that JFK was preparing for his own death 104 days later as he prayerfully watched over his struggling newborn second son. When Patrick expired, Kennedy's comment actually announced his own epitaph: "He was a fighter who gave life all he had." The President's faithful younger brother Bobby and his sister-in-law Lee Bouvier Radziwill joined John F. Kennedy for Patrick's private funeral Mass in the personal chapel of Boston's Cardinal Richard Cushing on August 10, 1963. They noted that humility seemed mysteriously attached to JFK like a badge of honor. A man of destiny, Jack Kennedy proved once again that he had surrendered to the inscrutable mystery of Divine Providence as he returned to his presidential duties.[196]

On September 24, 1963, the Senate passed a limited nuclear test ban treaty. In spite of best efforts by US Ambassador Henry Cabot Lodge, corruption continued to escalate in South Vietnam. Few were surprised on November 1, 1963, when Diem and his brother were brutally assassinated. JFK, however, was deeply troubled for many reasons by the all-too human foibles that facilitated the murder of the leader of South Vietnam.[197] Though regime change occurred, a prophetic inferno would arise out of festering Communist embers burning throughout Vietnam.[198]

American heroes are tempered in a cauldron of fire that never blazes low. John Eisenhower said of his famous father, undeniably a war hero and tactical leader like few among men, that in his declining years, Dwight D. Eisenhower was outspoken about the inherent wastefulness and cruelty of war. Esteemed military leaders with whom Kennedy personally worked, and perhaps inspired by his leadership, would ultimately agree that they were more against engaging combat troops to solve international disputes than were politicians who had never experienced firsthand the horrors of war. On JFK's watch, the Joint Chiefs of Staff resigned themselves to the inevitability of JFK's aversion to war, even in hot spots like Southeast Asia, although others continued to lobby for more troops in the region.[199]

John F. Kennedy is remembered as a calm and deliberate man of sincere leadership. Presidential counselor Ted Sorensen wrote that "[JFK] . . . was a natural leader. When he walked into a room, he became its center. When he spoke, people stopped and listened. When he grinned, even on television, viewers smiled back at him. He was much the same man in private as he was

THE HAND OF FATE STRIKES

in public. It was no act—the secret of his magic appeal was that he had no magic at all. But he did have charisma. Historians still write about it. Charisma is often in the eye of the beholder, and that was particularly true in Kennedy's case. It had to be experienced to be believed. It wasn't only his looks or his words; it was a special lightness of manner, the irony, the teasing, the self-effacement, the patient letting things be. Although he could be steely and stern when frustrated, he never lost his temper. When times were bad, he knew they would get better—when they were good, he knew they could get worse."[200] Vietnam was a place where JFK planned for times to get better. And so, they have. But at what human cost?

Education in the trades, as well as in science, engineering, mathematics, technology, history, law, medicine, literature, linguistics, geopolitics, military strategy, archeology, architecture, religion, sociology, psychology, spirituality, and the arts, all coupled with travel and communication among the varied cultures of the earth's populations bring deeper understanding of the value of a universal golden rule: do unto others as you would have them do unto you. The golden rule, however, often presumes that humankind is capable of judging what others need or want at any given time. Most would agree that such is not always the case. Now, responsible technological networking throughout the world can present opportunities for global expression of the inherent human rights everyone seeks.

Throughout much of his life, John F. Kennedy did not view his physical ailments as personal deterrents because of his staunch, unbending belief in the abiding goodness of Divine Providence, the Great Spirit within him, around him, and always with him: that same Great Spirit people of all times and places recognize but identify in differing linguistic expressions. Believing he was made in the Great Spirit's image and likeness, Christian JFK did his utmost to fashion his life choices as similarly as his situated freedom allowed. He had caring parents and siblings who encouraged and strengthened him along the way. His wife was strong, intuitive, and filled with love for him as he was with her. Kennedy believed the Great Spirit, well known to America's founding father George Washington and his peers, and even to Native Americans of the day, was indeed humankind's all-loving Father, Son, and Holy Spirit—One Being, the supreme Creator of Heaven and Earth, who redeemed humankind by His only begotten Son, Jesus Christ, at great price on Golgotha and sustains them on earth by His Spirit for a higher purpose than mere ego gratification. Committed Christian Kennedy was quite private about his faith. He was unafraid of suffering for he well knew not only its rawness but also, its value when united with Christ. Those who were close to him never doubted that JFK believed the most significant event in all human history is the effect of the humble Virgin Mary's willing consent to the Divine Will. Her hero boy Child would forever be acknowledged on earth as Jesus, the long-awaited Christ whose followers are as numerous as the stars of Heaven and as the desert and ocean sands. Though scandal attached to the Kennedy family even in JFK's time, his faith assured him that multitudes cheered him on.[201] Kennedy trusted Divine Providence to the best of his ability. Like the folks at the biblical wedding feast of Cana, John F. Kennedy, a child of Mary from his mom's womb, believed Mary's intercession would always help him.[202]

THE HAND OF FATE STRIKES

The Founders of the American Republic were unashamedly followers of the "Great Spirit" even though a few adopted the popular and erudite term "deist" to define themselves publicly.[203] The American Founders believed in the inherent human dignity of honorable people for which Jesus died on the cross. Like Jesus, the American Founders would openly lay down their fortunes, their sacred honor, indeed their very lives for their personal liberty, an inherent right flowing forth from Divinity.[204] The American Founders quietly comprehended that human liberty has a divine origin sanctified by Mary's hero Boy-Child, Jesus. Such patriots would form a new nation carved out of the frontiers of the wilderness on the American continent and defend it from generation to generation with every fiber of their being. The Christian cry: "Give me liberty or give me death" would awaken Herculean heroism in each patriotic American until the end.[205]

John F. Kennedy, always the sickly second son of old Boston's Irish Catholic Christians Rose and Joe, heard liberty's call deep in the wilderness of each illness he overcame. That providential call had served Jack Kennedy with ample time to read, think, and even to write books that shed light on the power of human weakness freely harnessed with the majesty of liberty's divine righteousness. No one knows how many times, if any, John F. Kennedy may have pondered the scripture verse: *Take my yoke upon you and learn from me, for I am gentle and humble of heart, and you will find rest for your souls. For my yoke is easy and my burden is light.*[206] Though perplexing empathy grows out of seeds of suffering all humankind must plant on earth, the winds of chaos sow strength in human roots that are deep in faith. And so, it must be for every honorable human who appreciates the burden of liberty's light.

John F. Kennedy lived much of his earth life enclosed in a body riddled with suffering. His bodily ailments became reminders of his noble calling. For unknown reasons, he was anointed with the mysterious hand of fate, Divine Providence. When the scriptural cloak fell upon him, it activated power and authority within and around John F. Kennedy.[207] On his watch, Armageddon would not flow out of the tiny island on the American continent known as Cuba. Honest history must therefore reflect that the hand of fate, a Kind Providence, guided John F. Kennedy's spiritual journey that preserved human life on earth for a while.

In late autumn of 1963, JFK's reelection to a second presidential term triggered heightened awareness of the fickle nature of most US voters. Conservatives thought Kennedy was soft on Communism and would not consider voting for him. Southern Democrats disliked his civil rights stance. Embracing his limitations and shortcomings like a marathon runner who pauses momentarily to catch a breath of air, JFK continued to run the race with alacrity and speed few recognized as he passed into history. Ever the pragmatist, Kennedy agreed to a fundraising campaign in Texas with feuding Texas Governor John Connally and Texas native Lyndon Johnson, his vice president.

JFK, who occasionally broached the subject of assassination during his contentious three years in office, seemed particularly preoccupied with that specter during his Texas trip. There was good reason for his awareness of his impending death.[208] In the weeks preceding his Dallas visit, Kennedy was informed of two

THE HAND OF FATE STRIKES

serious assassination plots against him. It would later be recognized that Kennedy was, in fact, being methodically stalked in the final weeks of his life.[209] Although Jacqueline was somewhat aware of clear and present danger to her husband, true love knows no bounds. Having served the United States together faithfully during their entire marriage, in sickness and in health, in the best of times and the worst of times, Jacqueline Kennedy had gladly agreed to accompany her beloved husband on his Texas campaign journey.

During ten years of marriage, courageous Jacqueline bore five of John F. Kennedy's children; four were delivered by body-draining caesarian surgery. She and President Kennedy suffered the loss of one stillborn child, the deaths of two others, and had two surviving children. In spite of painful sorrows, Jacqueline Bouvier Kennedy had previously accompanied her husband on presidential journeys to France, Austria, the United Kingdom, Italy, Venezuela, Mexico, Costa Rica, and Columbia. The First Lady also represented the US Presidency in Pakistan and India. Educated, refined, and exquisitely knowledgeable, Mrs. John F. Kennedy, accomplished the refurbishing of the White House as a historical edifice. She obtained authentic period furnishings and procured an endowment to preserve the historical integrity of the President's home. Jacqueline Kennedy, like her beloved husband, proved a faithful American leader of the finest caliber.

The hand of fate, mysteriously a Kind Providence, carefully taught JFK's wife painful lessons her husband perhaps knew well: to everything there is a season, and a time to every purpose under the heaven. There is a time to plant and to sow, and there is a time to be born and a time to die.[210] A beautiful woman of many talents, having drunk deep of the cup of sorrow laced with elation, Jacqueline Kennedy had charmed leaders worldwide. Remembering the Basilica of Our Lady of Guadalupe in Mexico City where the First Couple had worshipped near the miraculous tilma of Saint Juan Diego, America's First Lady Jacqueline Kennedy believed she and her beloved husband traveled in the providential care of the Blessed Virgin Mary, Mother of all the Living.[211] Her faith reminded her that Christian life is eternal.[212]

Both the President and the First Lady were aware that death threats abounded in Texas.[213] Dallas, however, was identified as a particularly dangerous location. JFK's response to assassination rumors and prophesies was noted by associates: "Simply accepting death as an inevitable fact of life, and simply recognizing assassination as an unavoidable hazard of the presidency, he refused to worry about his personal safety—not with any bravado or braggadocio but with an almost fatalist unconcern for danger . . . He mentioned more than once—but almost in passing—that no absolute protection was possible, that a determined assassin could always find a way, and that a sniper from a high window or rooftop seemed to him the least preventable."[214] Kennedy, ever the grandson of Boston's beloved Mayor Honey Fitz, usually waded into uncontrollable crowds of hand shakers and well-wishers at home and abroad "not to prove his courage, but because it was his job."[215]

The youthful US President and his beautiful First Lady were admired globally. Texas was no exception. When they arrived in San Antonio, Houston, and Fort Worth on November 21, 1963, enthusiastic crowds welcomed them. On that final morning of his life, the Democratic candidate for reelection Jack

THE HAND OF FATE STRIKES

Kennedy was elated when his glamorous wife, Jackie, attired in a pink Chanel suit and wearing white gloves, received a standing ovation from 2,000 Southern business executives and their spouses assembled in a Fort Worth hotel ballroom. Three months earlier, their sorrow had been deep as they together suffered the struggle and death of their beloved newborn second son Patrick. Now, the contagiously joyful US President and his beaming wife epitomized transmissible happiness that comes from a mysterious inner place known only to Divine Providence. JFK said to his lovely, affirming wife: "We're heading into nut country today . . . But Jackie, if somebody wants to shoot me from a window with a rifle, nobody can stop it, so why worry about it."[216]

At that time in American history, public display of affection was considered gauche, totally improper. For only a moment, as the First Couple were departing their hotel, Jack Kennedy tenderly brushed against his cherished wife with intimacy only they understood. Awaiting them, a highly enthusiastic crowd had gathered around the hotel exit to bid them farewell. JFK smiled warmly as he thanked them for their attendance. He reassured them of the need for the US to be first in space exploration and unmatched in defense. On that rainy morning in Fort Worth, few would forget what became known as John F. Kennedy's passionate final request: he asked everyone to accept courage that flows from leadership on behalf of the less fortunate. The more we have, the more we can give—for grace that is sourced in the Great Spirit is infinite.[217] Jacqueline knowingly smiled as she linked her arm through his.

The Presidential party efficiently departed the hotel and travelled by motorcade to Carswell Airforce Base where they boarded Air Force One for the thirteen-minute flight to Dallas. The Kennedy group was warmly welcomed when they landed at Love Field in Dallas. Onlookers cheered as Mrs. Kennedy was presented with a bouquet of blood red roses. The President quietly noted that Jacqueline had received bouquets of yellow roses at other venues across the state.[218] After greeting the crowds gathered at Love Field, the President and Mrs. Kennedy got into an awaiting open-top convertible for the ten-mile drive to downtown Dallas. Cheering, waving crowds lined each side of the streets they passed. Approximately five minutes before the motorcade reached the Dallas Triple Underpass, some in the crowds heard shots ring out. Photos captured the exuberant US President lunge forward before falling into his wife's lap. Shortly thereafter, a Catholic priest administered the Christian sacramental Last Rites for the fifth and final time to US President John F. Kennedy at nearby Parkland Memorial Hospital.[219] The thirty-fifth President of the United States was officially pronounced dead immediately afterward. He was forty-six years old.

As news of Kennedy's assassination spread around the world, tears, rage, and sorrow as deep as scriptural hell descended over the earth like a heavy cloud of pain bearing no quick remedy. If there were those who rejoiced, they were quiet for a while. In life and death, John F. Kennedy had effectively broken through the prejudice of generations who found Catholic Christianity distasteful. Divine Providence used him, with his consent, to reveal that faith steeped in education, refinement, fortitude, and graciousness in defeat spawn righteousness that has power and illumination to recognize the inherent human need for dignity steeped in liberty. JFK epitomized the delight of loving family,

THE HAND OF FATE STRIKES

the sacrificial stability of sacramental marriage, the pleasure of financial adequacy, and most of all, enduring belief in the faithfulness of an all-loving Kind Providence: a Savior both human and divine who knows all things, can do all things, and loves everyone unconditionally in spite of, or perhaps because of, the choices he or she makes. John F. Kennedy's accomplishments showed that sickness, weakness, pain, and sorrow are not impediments to the higher elements of peace on earth sourced in the divine imperative of human liberty. Rather, properly discerned difficulties are like a propeller that generates the motivation peace on earth demands of those who seek life, liberty and the pursuit of happiness.

Nikita Khruschev wrote in his memoirs of Kennedy's assassination: ". . . his death was a great loss. He was gifted with the ability to resolve international conflicts by negotiations . . . he was a real statesman. I believe that if Kennedy had lived, relations between the Soviet Union and the United States would be much better than they are."[220]

The body of John F. Kennedy was immediately transported back to Washington aboard Air Force One. His widow remained by his casket that had been placed in the cargo section of the plane. Her pink Chanel suit was stained with her dead husband's blood. Indeed, the bloodstains showed photo-snapping photographers, in Jacqueline's words, "what they did to him." She decided that JFK's funeral would be similar to that of slain US President Abraham Lincoln a hundred years earlier. President Kennedy's flag-draped casket would be transported to the Capitol on a caisson drawn by six grey horses, accompanied by one riderless black horse.

Streets along the way were lined with weeping mourners. During the twenty-one hours that JFK's body lay in state in the Capitol Rotunda, upwards of 250,000 passed by to pay their respects. In spite of many death threats against him, the aged World War II French hero, Charles de Gaulle, at six feet, five inches tall, chose to stand in John F. Kennedy's honor during the entire Solemn Requiem Mass at Saint Matthews Cathedral in Washington, DC. He stood respectfully in the presence of three other leaders representing the Western powers: Prime Minister Harold Macmillan, Prince Philip of Great Britain, and Ludwig Erhard of West Germany. Of course, the full Washington diplomatic corps and DC notables were all present as well.

On Monday, November 25, 1963, John F. Kennedy's remains were interred at Arlington National Cemetery where war heroes are laid to rest. Mrs. Kennedy and her husband's two brothers lit an eternal flame at the grave site; a symbol of the spirit of luminous liberty that cannot be extinguished as long as humans exist.

* * *

The assassination of JFK would break blustering Nikita Khruschev's heart. It was reported in late November: "Hearing the news from Dallas, Khruschev broke down and sobbed in the Kremlin. He took the news as a personal blow . . . For several days he was unable to perform his duties. Khruschev was convinced that Kennedy was killed by militaristic forces bent on sabotaging the two leaders' efforts to reach détente . . . Together, they were staking out a course that was steering the two countries away from nuclear brinkmanship to a new world

THE HAND OF FATE STRIKES

harmony."[221] Less than a year later, a bloodless coup occurred in the Soviet Union. Nikita Khruschev was overthrown by hardliner Leonard Brezhnev. Khruschev wrote his memoirs, which were smuggled out of Russia to the West where his book became a bestseller.[222] He referred to John F. Kennedy as a real statesman despite his youth. Nikita Khruschev believed that if JFK had lived, and with his help, he and John F. Kennedy could have finally brought peace to the earth.[223] Fidel Castro was stunned as news of the assassination of John F. Kennedy reached him. The Cuban leader had observed that historically, JFK had the possibility of becoming the greatest president of the United States.[224]

The Catholic Archbishop at Mexico City authorized a Requiem Mass in honor of the fallen US President at the Basilica Shrine of Our Lady of Guadalupe where President John F. Kennedy and the First Lady had occupied the front pew during their official visit to Mexico in June of 1962, worshipping alongside Mexico's faithful who would now pay their final respects to their fellow pilgrim. There were authorized Requiem Masses at the Shrines of Lourdes and Fatima where seekers would honor the soul of a man who had helped rescue their nations from the frightening tenacles of nuclear Armageddon.

Washington's Auxiliary Bishop Philip Hannan, who had earned a Doctorate Degree in Canon Law in Rome as a young man, was at the Vatican attending the Second Ecumenical Council where the slain US President's views were well respected when news of Kennedy's assassination reached him. Hannan was a confidante of both the First Lady and US President John F. Kennedy. Many years later, the retired Archbishop of New Orleans, Louisiana, Phillip Hannan said his memory would always be filled with awe as he sat with the author recalling the unfathomable tenderness and love JFK and his wife Jacqueline shared for one another. Of course, knowledgeable as he was concerning many mysteries within the ancient Church of Rome, the Archbishop recognized divine love—the humanly unknowable hand of fate, Divine Providence guiding John F. Kennedy and his beautiful Jacqueline's sacramental marriage away from earth's defilements. Elderly Archbishop Hannan would describe how he missed his friend Jack Kennedy. A professed child of Mary himself, scholar-soldier Archbishop Hannon wrote: "I still marvel that God saw fit to bring John Kennedy and me into each other's lives at that particular moment in American history. In the end, I have only the most inexpressible wonder and gratitude for having enjoyed such a remarkable relationship with such a remarkable man—one of America's truly great leaders . . . Despite our national broken hearts, the machinery of democracy neither fell apart nor ground to a halt [at his assassination], providing, instead, one of the finest hours in our national history."[225]

There indeed was a modest brilliance to JFK's administration. Many peers believed that JFK was a martyr who died for a cause. They are not alone in that assessment. A knowledgeable Paris-based American journalist admitted on the record: "I think Kennedy died for something . . . Any man is measured by his enemies. It must never be forgotten that he went to Dallas to confront [his enemies] . . . to tell the people of that city, of the nation, and the world beyond, that peace is not a sign of weakness."[226] Though his earth life was finished, assassinated US President John F. Kennedy had completed his earth

THE HAND OF FATE STRIKES

assignments dressed in fate's mysterious wisdom that perhaps flowed throughout the world from Fatima, a tiny hamlet in the towering mountains of Portugal. Perhaps the prayers and sacrifices of unseen multitudes who responded to Fatima's graces sustained the frightened populations of the earth during the Cuban Missile Crisis. Ours is not to know but only to reason why.

JFK dared to humanize the aggressively dangerous leader of the Soviet Union, Nikita Khruschev, reminding everyone of decency in all times and places about deadly fires on earth caused by nuclear weapons of mass destruction. John F. Kennedy reminded peers in his famous Peace Speech at American University shortly before his murder: "We all inhabit this small planet. We all breathe the same air. We all cherish our children's future. And we are all mortal." Jack Kennedy's humanity lives on in the minds and memories and hearts of all leaders who pursue liberty on earth. The prism of hindsight recognizes JFK's stalwart faith in the ideals of America's Founders. His leadership grew out of his unshakable trust that all things work together for good for those who are called.[227] John F. Kennedy used his life's circumstances to refine immortal decency in himself that those of honest conscience must admire.

When scripture's providential cloak fell upon him, Rose and Joe Kennedy's agony-ridden second son did not pull back. Instead, he freely chose in deed and word to become a symbolic flame of hope sourced in American liberty's ideals.[228] Fleeting flickers from the past stimulated silent sounds of hurrying hoofbeats of long-gone heroes heard by JFK, a world leader who looked deep into liberty's lure on behalf of humankind. Long ago, when John F. Kennedy lived, served, and was slaughtered for a cause we may never really know or even understand, the long lens of history makes clear that he, like his parents, grandparents, and immigrant ancestors before them, along with his soon-to-be widowed wife, Jacqueline, were indeed martyrs for love who graciously accepted their (invisible) crosses (of duty) because they loved beyond their natural capacity. Their martyrdom was offering their lives, their fortunes and their sacred honor for hallowed liberty smoldering within their patriotic American heritage. Consequently, they did for others what others had done for them.[229] No one of decency can ask for more.

Jack Kennedy personally renounced himself, took up his ailing, pain-consumed body, and transformed by duty steeped in love higher than himself, showed to all the world by his journey to Dallas, Texas the salvific power of liberty that Jesus exhibited during his crucifixion on Golgotha. To this day, liberty's intoxicating lure envelopes humankind in light. John F. Kennedy showed people of all times and places that patriotic martyrdom—offering one's life in fulfillment of liberty's just call—is the highest duty of humankind.

John F. Kennedy's gravesite bears an actual flame at Arlington National Cemetery that memorializes American liberty glowing from the invisible hand of fate; Divine Providence shepherding the earth's population to a promised land beyond every cloud of unknowing. Jack Kennedy, the faithful American leader, who willingly rode to his death in the back seat of a Lincoln convertible, surrendered his human spirit to the "Great Spirit" who guides all that is and was and ever will be honorable on earth as it is in Heaven. The thirty-fifth President of the United States had finished the race; he had kept the faith.[230] Wise patriots throughout the world realize he had found the biblical pearl of great price.[231] John F. Kennedy gave his life to preserve such treasure for everyone of goodwill.

APPENDIX ONE

Inaugural Address of John F. Kennedy
January 20, 1961

"Vice President Johnson, Mr. Speaker, Mr. Chief Justice, President Eisenhower, Vice President Nixon, President Truman, Reverend Clergy, fellow citizens:

We observe today not a victory of party but a celebration of freedom—symbolizing an end as well as a beginning—signifying renewal as well as change. For I have sworn before you and Almighty God the same solemn oath our forebears prescribed nearly a century and three-quarters ago.

The world is very different now. For man holds in his mortal hands the power to abolish all forms of human poverty and all forms of human life. And yet the same revolutionary beliefs for which our forebears fought are still at issue around the globe—the belief that the rights of man come not from the generosity of the state but from the hand of God.

We dare not forget today that we are the heirs of that first revolution. Let the word go forth from this time and place, to friend and foe alike, that the torch has been passed to a new generation of Americans—born in this century, tempered by war, disciplined by a hard and bitter peace, proud of our ancient heritage—and unwilling to witness or permit the slow undoing of those human rights to which this nation has always been committed, and to which we are committed today at home and around the world.

Let every nation know, whether it wishes us well or ill, that we shall pay any price, bear any burden, meet any hardship, support any friend, oppose any foe to assure the survival and the success of liberty.

This much we pledge—and more.

To those old allies, whose cultural and spiritual origins we share, we pledge the loyalty of faithful friends. United there is little we cannot do in a host of cooperative ventures. Divided there is little we can do—for we dare not meet a powerful challenge at odds and split asunder.

To those new states whom we welcome to the ranks of the free, we pledge our word that one form of colonial control shall not have passed away merely to be replaced by a far more iron tyranny. We shall not always expect to find them supporting our view. But we shall always hope to find them strongly supporting their own freedom—and to remember that, in the past, those who foolishly sought power by riding the back of the tiger ended up inside.

To those people in the huts and villages of half the globe struggling to break the bonds of mass misery, we pledge our best efforts to help them help themselves, for whatever period is required—not because the communists may be doing it, not because we seek their votes, but because it is right. If a free society cannot help the many who are poor, it cannot save the few who are rich.

To our sister republics south of our border, we offer a special pledge—to convert our good words into good deeds—in a new alliance for progress—to assist free men and free governments in casting off the chains of poverty. But this peaceful revolution of hope cannot become the prey of hostile powers. Let all our neighbors know that we shall join with them to oppose aggression or subversion anywhere in the Americas. And let every other power know that this hemisphere intends to remain the master of its own house.

To that world assembly of sovereign states, the United Nations, our last best hope in an age where the instruments of war have far outpaced the instruments of peace, we renew our pledge of support—to prevent it from becoming merely a forum for invective—to strengthen its shield of the new and the weak—and to enlarge the area in which its writ may run.

Finally, to those nations who would make themselves our adversary, we offer not a pledge but a request: that both sides begin anew the quest for peace, before the dark powers of destruction unleashed by science engulf all humanity in planned or accidental self-destruction.

We dare not tempt them with weakness. For only when our arms are sufficient beyond doubt can we be certain beyond doubt that they will never be employed.

But neither can two great and powerful groups of nations take comfort from our present course—both sides overburdened by the cost of modern weapons, both rightly alarmed by the steady spread of the deadly atom, yet both racing to alter that uncertain balance of terror that stays the hand of mankind's final war.

So let us begin anew—remembering on both sides that civility is not a sign of weakness, and sincerity is always subject to proof. Let us never negotiate out of fear. But let us never fear to negotiate.

Let both sides explore what problems unite us instead of belaboring those problems which divide us.

Let both sides, for the first time, formulate serious and precise proposals for the inspection and control of arms—and bring the absolute power to destroy other nations under the absolute control of all nations.

Let both sides seek to invoke the wonders of science instead of its terrors. Together let us explore the stars, conquer the deserts, eradicate disease, tap the ocean depths, and encourage the arts and commerce.

Let both sides unite to heed in all corners of the earth the command of Isaiah—to 'undo the heavy burdens . . .(and) let the oppressed go free.'

And if a beachhead of cooperation may push back the jungle of suspicion, let both sides join in creating a new endeavor, not a new balance of power, but a new world of law, where the strong are just and the weak secure and the peace preserved.

All this will not be finished in the first one hundred days. Nor will it be finished in the first one thousand days, nor in the life of this administration, nor even perhaps in our lifetime on this planet. But let us begin.

In your hands, my fellow citizens, more than mine, will rest the final success or failure of our course. Since this country was founded, each generation of Americans has been summoned to give testimony to its national loyalty. The graves of young

Americans who answered the call to service surround the globe.

Now the trumpet summons us again—not as a call to bear arms, though arms we need—not as a call to battle, though embattled we are—but a call to bear the burden of a long twilight struggle, year in and year out, 'rejoicing in hope, patient in tribulation'—a struggle against the common enemies of man: tyranny, poverty, disease, and war itself.

Can we forge against these enemies a grand and global alliance, north and south, east and west, that can assure a more fruitful life for all mankind? Will you join in that historic effort?

In the long history of the world, only a few generations have been granted the role of defending freedom in its hour of maximum danger. I do not shrink from this responsibility—I welcome it. I do not believe that any of us would exchange places with any other people or any other generation. The energy, the faith, the devotion which we bring to this endeavor will light our country and all who serve it—and the glow from that fire can truly light the world.

And so, my fellow Americans: ask not what your country can do for you—ask what you can do for your country.

My fellow citizens of the world: ask not what America will do for you, but what together we can do for the freedom of man.

Finally, whether you are citizens of America or citizens of the world, ask of us here the same high standards of strength and sacrifice which we ask of you. With a good conscience our only sure reward, with history the final judge of our deeds, let us go forth to lead the land we love, asking His blessing and His help, but knowing that here on earth God's work must truly be our own."[232]

APPENDIX TWO

Life Consecration to Jesus Christ

All humans are born of sacrificial mothers who subject their bodies to pain and sickness at the hand of fate as they bring forth humans destined for the Heavenly Kingdom. Motherhood, like fatherhood, is a divine calling. Jesus Christ distinctly revealed the Divine Fatherhood all humans enjoy.[233] He alone reveals the Heavenly Father of humankind.[234] Jesus Christ dying on His cross of redemption for all people of all denominations and religions from the beginning to the end said to the loyal disciple who loved Him: "Behold thy Mother, and to His sorrowful Mother Mary—Behold thy son."[235] Those who identify themselves as "children of Mary" for the love of Jesus rest secure in her care too, as Christ revealed at the wedding feast of Cana.[236]

I, _____ , a faithless sinner, renew and ratify today in thy hands, O pure Virgin Mary, the vows of my baptism; I renounce forever Satan, his displays, and works; and I give myself entirely to Jesus Christ, the Incarnate Wisdom, to carry my cross after Him all the days of my life, and to be more faithful to Him than I have ever been before. In the presence of all the heavenly court, I choose thee this day for my Mother and Mistress. I deliver and consecrate to thee, as thy slave, my body and soul, my goods, both interior and exterior, and even the value of all my good actions, past, present, and future; leaving to thee the entire and full right of disposing of me, and all that belongs to me, without exception, according to thy good pleasure, for the greater glory of God in time and in eternity. Amen.[237]

APPENDIX THREE

The Midnight Ride of Paul Revere

"Listen, my children, and you shall hear
Of the midnight ride of Paul revere,
On the eighteenth of April, in seventy-five:
Hardly a man is now alive
Who remembers that famous day and year.
He said to his friend, 'If the British march
By Land or sea from the town to-night,
Hang a lantern aloft in the belfry-arch
Of the North Church tower, as a signal light.
One is by land, and two if by sea:
And I on the opposite shore will be,
Ready to ride and spread the alarm
Through every Middlesex village and farm
For the country—folk to up and to arm.'
Then he said, 'Good night!' and with muffled oar
Silently rowed to the Charlestown shore,
Just as the moon rose over the bay,
Where swinging wide at her moorings lay

THE SPIRITUAL LEGACY OF JOHN F. KENNEDY

The Somerset, British man-of-war:
A phantom ship, with each mast and spar
Across the moon, like a prison-bar,
And a huge black hulk, that was magnified
By its own reflection in the tide.
Meanwhile, his friend, through alley and street
Wanders and watches with eager ears,
Till in the silence around him he hears
The muster of men at the barrack door,
The sound of arms, and the tramp of feet,
And the measured tread of the grenadiers
Marching down to their boats on the shore.
Then he climbed to the tower of the church,
Up the wooden stairs, with stealthy tread,
To the belfry-chamber overhead,
And startled the pigeons from their perch
On the somber rafters, that round him made
Masses and moving shapes of shade,
By the trembling ladder, steep and tall,
To the highest window in the wall,
Where he pause to listen and look down
A moment on the roofs of the town,
And the moonlight flowing over all.
Beneath, in the churchyard, lay the dead,
In their night-encampment on the hill,
Wrapped in silence so deep and still
That he could hear, like a sentinel's tread,
The watchful night-wind, as it went
Creeping along from tent to tent,

THE MIDNIGHT RIDE OF PAUL REVERE

And seeming to whisper, 'All is well!'
A moment only he feels the spell
Of the place and the hour, and the secret dread
Of the lonely belfry and the dead.
For suddenly all his thoughts are bent
On a shadowy something far away,
Where the river widens to meet the bay,
And a line of black, that bends and floats
On the rising tide, like a bridge of boats.
Meanwhile, impatient to mount and ride,
Booted and spurred, with a heavy stride,
On the opposite shore walked Paul Revere.
Now he patted his horse's side,
Now gazed on the landscape far and near,
Then impetuous stamped the earth,
And turned and tightened his saddle-girth.
But mostly he watched with eager search
The belfry-tower of the old north church,
And it rose above the graves on the hill,
Lonely and spectral and somber and still.
And lo! As he looks, on the belfry's height,
A glimmer, and then a gleam of light!
Her springs to the saddle, the bridle he turns,
But lingers and gazes, till full on his sight
A second lamp in the belfry burns!
A hurry of hoofs in a visage street,
A shape in the moonlight, a bulk in the dark,
And beneath from the pebbles, in
Passing, a spark

Struck out by a steed that flies fearless and fleet:
That was all! And yet, through the gloom and the light,
The fate of a nation was riding that night.
And the spark struck out by that steed, in his flight,
Kindled the land into flame with its heat.
He has left the village and mounted the steep,
And beneath him, tranquil and broad and deep,
In the mystic, meeting the ocean tides.
And under the alders, that skirt its doe,
Now soft on the sand, now loud on the ledge,
Is heard the tramp of his steed as he rides.
It was twelve by the village clock
When he crossed the bridge into Medford town.
He heard the crowing of the cock,
And the barking of the famer's dog,
And felt the damp of the river-fog,
That rises when the sun goes down.
It was one by the village clock,
When he galloped into Lexington.
He saw the gilded weathercock
Swim in the moonlight as he passed,
And the meeting-house windows, blank and bare,
Gaze at him with spectral glare,
As if they already stood aghast
At the bloody work they would look upon.
It was two by the village clock,
When he came to the bridge in Concord town.
He heard the bleating of the flock,
And the twitter of birds among the trees,

THE MIDNIGHT RIDE OF PAUL REVERE

And felt the breath of the morning breeze
Blowing over the meadows brown.
And one was safe and asleep in his bed
Who at the bridge would be first to fall,
Who that day would be lying dead,
Pierced by a British musket-ball. You know the rest.
In the books you have read,
How the British Regulars fired and fled,
—How the farmers gave them ball for ball,
From behind each fence and farmyard-wall,
Chasing the red coats down the lane,
Then crossing the fields to emerge again
Under the trees at the turn of the road,
And only pausing to fire and load.
So, through the night rode Paul Revere.
And so, through the night went his cry of alarm
To every Middlesex village and farm,
—A cry of defiance, and not of fear,
A voice in the darkness, a knock at the door,
And a word what shall echo forevermore!
For, borne on the night-wind of the past,
Through all our history, to the last,
In the hour of darkness and peril and need,
The people will waken and listen to hear
The hurrying hoof-beats of that steed
And the midnight message of Paul Revere.[238]

APPENDIX FOUR

Peace

"Peace is a process - a way of solving problems."[239]

"There are few earthly things more beautiful than a university," wrote John Masefield in his tribute to English universities—and his words are equally true today. He did not refer to spires and towers, to campus greens and ivied walls. He admired the splendid beauty of the university, he said, because it was "a place where those who hate ignorance may strive to know, where those who perceive truth may strive to make others see."

I have, therefore, chosen this time and this place to discuss a topic on which ignorance too often abounds and the truth is too rarely perceived—yet it is the most important topic on earth: world peace.

What kind of peace do I mean? What kind of peace do we seek? Not a Pax Americana enforced on the world by American weapons of war. Not the peace of the grave or the security of the slave. I am talking about genuine peace, the kind of peace that makes life on earth worth living, the kind that enables men and nations to grow and to hope and to build a better life for their children—not merely peace for Americans but peace for all men and women—not merely peace in our time but peace for all time.

I speak of peace because of the new face of war. Total war makes no sense in an age when great powers can maintain large and relatively invulnerable nuclear forces and refuse to surrender without resort to those forces. It makes no sense in an age when a single nuclear weapon contains almost ten times the explosive force delivered by all the allied air forces in the Second World War. It makes no sense in an age when the deadly poisons produced by a nuclear exchange would be carried by wind and water and soil and seed to the far corners of the globe and to generations yet unborn.

Today the expenditure of billions of dollars every year on weapons acquired for the purpose of making sure we never need to use them is essential to keeping the peace. But surely the acquisition of such idle stockpiles—which can only destroy and never create—is not the only, much less the most efficient, means of assuring peace.

I speak of peace, therefore, as the necessary rational end of rational men. I realize that the pursuit of peace is not as dramatic as the pursuit of war—and frequently the words of the pursuer fall on deaf ears. But we have no more urgent task.

Some say that it is useless to speak of world peace or world law or world disarmament—and that it will be useless until the leaders of the Soviet Union adopt a more enlightened attitude. I hope they do. I believe we can help them do it. But I also believe that we must reexamine our own attitude—as individuals and as a nation—for our attitude is as essential as theirs. And every graduate of this school, every thoughtful citizen who despairs of war and wishes to bring peace, should begin by looking inward—by examining his own attitude toward the possibilities of peace, toward the Soviet Union, toward the course of the Cold War, and toward freedom and peace here at home.

First: Let us examine our attitude toward peace itself. Too many of us think it is impossible. Too many think it unreal. But that is a dangerous, defeatist belief. It leads to the conclusion that war is inevitable—that mankind is doomed—that we are gripped by forces we cannot control.

We need not accept that view. Our problems are manmade—therefore, they can be solved by man. And man can be as big as he wants. No problem of human destiny is beyond human beings. Man's reason and spirit have often solved the seemingly unsolvable—and we believe they can do it again.

I am not referring to the absolute, infinite concept of peace and goodwill of which some fantasies and fanatics dream. I do not deny the value of hopes and dreams, but we merely invite discouragement and incredulity by making that our only and immediate goal.

Let us focus instead on a more practical, more attainable peace—based not on a sudden revolution in human nature but on a gradual evolution in human institutions—on a series of concrete actions and effective agreements which are in the interest of all concerned. There is no single, simple key to this peace—no grand or magic formula to be adopted by one or two powers. Genuine peace must be the product of many nations, the sum of many acts. It must be dynamic, not static, changing to meet the challenge of each new generation. For peace is a process—a way of solving problems.

With such a peace, there will still be quarrels and conflicting interests, as there are within families and nations. World peace, like community peace, does not require that each man love his neighbor—it requires only that they live together in mutual tolerance, submitting their disputes to a just and peaceful settlement. And history teaches us that enmities between nations, as between individuals, do not last forever. However fixed our likes and dislikes may seem, the tide of time and events will often bring surprising changes in the relations between nations and neighbors.

So let us persevere. Peace need not be impracticable, and war need not be inevitable. By defining our goal more clearly, by making it seem more manageable and less remote, we can help all peoples to see it, to draw hope from it, and to move irresistibly toward it.

Second: Let us reexamine our attitude toward the Soviet Union. It is discouraging to think that their leaders may actually believe what their propagandists write. It is discouraging to read a recent authoritative Soviet text on military strategy and find, on page after page, wholly baseless and incredible claims—such as the allegation that "American imperialist circles are preparing to unleash different types of wars . . . that there is a very real threat of a preventive war being unleashed by American imperialists against the Soviet Union . . . [and that] the political aims of the American imperialists are to enslave economically and politically the European and other capitalist countries . . . [and] to achieve world domination

... by means of aggressive wars."

Truly, as it was written long ago: "The wicked flee when no man pursueth." Yet it is sad to read these Soviet statements—to realize the extent of the gulf between us. But it is also a warning—a warning to the American people not to fall into the same trap as the Soviets, not to see only a distorted and desperate view of the other side, not to see conflict as inevitable, accommodation as impossible, and communication as nothing more than an exchange of threats.

No government or social system is so evil that its people must be considered as lacking in virtue. As Americans, we find communism profoundly repugnant as a negation of personal freedom and dignity. But we can still hail the Russian people for their many achievements—in science and space, in economic and industrial growth, in culture and in acts of courage.

Among the many traits the peoples of our two countries have in common, none is stronger than our mutual abhorrence of war. Almost unique among the major world powers, we have never been at war with each other. And no nation in the history of battle ever suffered more than the Soviet Union suffered in the course of the Second World War. At least twenty million lost their lives. Countless millions of homes and farms were burned or sacked. A third of the nation's territory, including nearly two thirds of its industrial base, was turned into a wasteland—a loss equivalent to the devastation of this country east of Chicago.

Today, should total war ever break out again—no matter how—our two countries would become the primary targets. It is an ironic but accurate fact that the two strongest powers are the two in the most danger of devastation. All we have built, all we have worked for, would be destroyed in the first twenty-four hours. And even in the Cold War, which brings burdens and dangers to so many nations, including this nation's closest allies—our two countries bear the heaviest burdens. For we are both devoting massive sums of money to weapons that could be better devoted to combating ignorance, poverty, and disease. We are both caught up in a vicious and dangerous cycle in which suspicion on one side breeds suspicion on the other, and new weapons beget counter weapons.

In short, both the United States and its allies, and the Soviet Union and its allies, have a mutually deep interest in a just and genuine peace and in halting the arms race. Agreements to this end are in the interests of the Soviet Union as well as ours—and even the most hostile nations can be relied upon to accept and keep those treaty obligations, and only those treaty obligations, which are in their own interest.

So, let us not be blind to our differences—but let us also direct attention to our common interests and to the means by which those differences can be resolved. And if we cannot end now our differences, at least we can help make the world safe for diversity. For, in the final analysis, our most basic common link is that we all inhabit this small planet. We all breathe the same air. We all cherish our children's future. And we are all mortal.

Third: Let us reexamine our attitude toward the Cold War, remembering that we are not engaged in a debate, seeking to pile up debating points. We are not here distributing blame or pointing the finger of judgment. We must deal with the world as it is, and not as it might have been had the history of the last eighteen years been different.

We must, therefore, persevere in the search for peace in the hope that constructive changes within the Communist Bloc might bring within reach solutions which now seem beyond us. We must conduct our affairs in such a way that it becomes in the Communists' interest to agree on a genuine peace. Above all, while defending our own vital interests, nuclear powers must avert those confrontations, which bring an adversary to a choice of either a humiliating retreat or a nuclear war. To adopt that kind of course in the nuclear age would be evidence only of the bankruptcy of our policy—or of a collective death wish for the world.

To secure these ends, America's weapons are nonprovocative, carefully controlled, designed to deter, and capable of selective use. Our military forces are committed to peace and disciplined in self-restraint. Our diplomats are instructed to avoid unnecessary irritants and purely rhetorical hostility.

For we can seek a relaxation of tension without relaxing our guard. And, for our part, we do not need to use threats to prove that we are resolute. We do not need to jam foreign broadcasts out of fear our faith will be eroded. We are unwilling to impose our system on any unwilling people—but we are willing and able to engage in peaceful competition with any people on earth.

Meanwhile, we seek to strengthen the United Nations, to help solve its financial problems, to make it a more effective instrument for peace, to develop it into a genuine world security system—a system capable of resolving disputes on the basis of law, of ensuring the security of the large and the small, and of creating conditions under which arms can finally be abolished.

At the same time, we seek to keep peace inside the non-Communist world, where many nations, all of them our friends, are divided over issues which weaken Western unity, which invite Communist intervention, or which threaten to erupt into war. Our efforts in West New Guinea, in Congo, in the Middle East, and in the Indian subcontinent, have been persistent and patient despite criticism from both sides. We have also tried to set an example for others—by seeking to adjust small but significant differences with our own closest neighbors in Mexico and in Canada.

Speaking of other nations, I wish to make one point clear. We are bound to many nations by alliances. Those alliances exist because our concern and theirs substantially overlap. Our commitment to defend Western Europe and West Berlin, for example, stands undiminished because of the identity of our vital interests. The United States will make no deal with the Soviet Union at the expense of other nations and other peoples, not merely because they are our partners, but also because their interests and ours converge.

Our interests converge, however, not only in defending the frontiers of freedom, but in pursuing the paths of peace. It is our hope—and the purpose of allied policies—to convince the Soviet Union that she, too, should let each nation choose its own future, so long as that choice does not interfere with the choices of others. The Communist drive to impose their political and economic system on others is the primary cause of world tension today. For there can be no doubt that, if all nations could refrain from interfering in the self-determination of others, the peace would be much more assured.

This will require a new effort to achieve world law—a new context for world discussions. It will require increased understanding between the Soviets and ourselves. And increased understanding will require increased contact and communication. One step in this direction is the proposed arrangement for a direct line between Moscow and Washington, to avoid on each side the dangerous delays, misunderstandings, and misreading of the other's actions, which might occur at a time of crisis.

We have also been talking in Geneva about the other first-step measures of arms control designed to limit the intensity of the arms race and to reduce the risks of accidental war. Our primary long-range interest in Geneva, however, is general and complete disarmament—designed to take place by stages, permitting parallel political developments to build the new institutions of peace, which would take the place of arms. The pursuit of disarmament has been an effort of this government since the 1920s. It has been urgently sought by the past three administrations. And however dim the prospects may be today, we intend to continue this effort—to continue it in order that all countries, including our own, can better grasp what the problems and possibilities of disarmament are.

The one major area of these negotiations where the end is in sight, yet where a fresh start is badly needed, is in a treaty to outlaw nuclear tests. The conclusion of such a treaty, so near and yet so far, would check the spiraling arms race in one of its most dangerous areas. It would place the nuclear powers in a position to deal more effectively with one of the greatest hazards which man faces in 1963, the further spread of nuclear arms. It would increase our security—it would decrease the prospects of war. Surely this goal is sufficiently important to require our steady pursuit, yielding neither to the temptation to give up the whole effort nor the temptation to give up our insistence on vital and responsible safeguards.

I am taking this opportunity, therefore, to announce two important decisions in this regard.

First: Chairman Khrushchev, Prime Minister Macmillan, and I have agreed that high-level discussions will shortly begin in Moscow looking toward early agreement on a comprehensive test ban treaty. Our hopes must be tempered with the caution of history—but with our hopes go the hopes of all mankind.

Second: To make clear our good faith and solemn convictions on the matter, I now declare that the United States does not propose to conduct nuclear tests in the atmosphere so long as other states do not do so. We will not be the first to resume. Such a declaration is no substitute for a formal binding treaty, but I hope it will help us achieve one. Nor would such a treaty be a substitute for disarmament, but I hope it will help us achieve it.

Finally, my fellow Americans, let us examine our attitude toward peace and freedom here at home. The quality and spirit of our own society must justify and support our efforts abroad. We must show it in the dedication of our own lives—as many of you who are graduating today will have a unique opportunity to do, by serving without pay in the Peace Corps abroad or in the proposed National Service Corps here at home.

But wherever we are, we must all, in our daily lives, live up to the age-old faith that peace and freedom walk together. In too many of our cities today, the peace is not secure because the freedom is incomplete.

It is the responsibility of the executive branch at all levels of government—local, state, and national—to provide and protect that freedom for all of our citizens by all means within their authority. It is the responsibility of the legislative branch at all levels, wherever that authority is not now adequate, to make it adequate. And it is the responsibility of all citizens in all sections of this country to respect the rights of all others and to respect the law of the land.

All this is not unrelated to world peace. "When a man's ways please the Lord," the scriptures tell us, "he maketh even his enemies to be at peace with him." And is not peace, in the last analysis, basically a matter of human rights—the right to live out our lives without fear of devastation—the right to breathe air as nature provided it—the right of future generations to a healthy existence?

While we proceed to safeguard our national interests, let us also safeguard human interests. And the elimination of war and arms is clearly in the interest of both. No treaty, however much it may be to the advantage of all, however tightly it may be worded, can provide absolute security against the risks of deception and evasion. But it can—if it is sufficiently effective in its enforcement and if it is sufficiently in the interests of its signers—offer far more security and far fewer risks than an unabated, uncontrolled, unpredictable arms race.

The United States, as the world knows, will never start a war. We do not want a war. We do not now expect a war. This generation of Americans has already had enough—more than enough—of war and hate and oppression. We shall be prepared if others wish it. We shall be alert to try to stop it. But we shall also do our part to build a world of peace where the weak are safe and the strong are just. We are not helpless before that task or hopeless of its success. Confident and unafraid, we labor on—not toward a strategy of annihilation but toward a strategy of peace.[240]

ACKNOWLEDGEMENTS

AMDG

Any good that comes from this work is totally attributable to Kind Providence.

Thérèse Martin and her dedicated colleagues contribute to all my work.

This work reflects my gratitude to all who struggle relentlessly to be peacemakers in whatever walk of life they find themselves.

I am deeply grateful to those who shared their memories of the thirty-fifth President of the United States but chose to remain anonymous. Their inspiration remains a lighthouse in dark times. Thank you.

Honorable military demonstrate what true Americans are and no one can thank them enough.

I especially thank the sacrificial theologians who through the years have guided my work. Thanks also belongs to the late Archbishop Philip Hannan who, as Auxiliary Bishop of Washington, DC, was spiritual director of both Jacqueline and John F. Kennedy during JFK's 1,000-day Presidency. The retired archbishop sat at our family kitchen table gently reminiscing about the brilliant love story of John F. Kennedy and his devoted wife Jacqueline as he reflected on their unstinting dedication to their Catholic Christian faith and to the nation.

The John F. Kennedy Library in Boston preserves invaluable historical data and insights into the spirit of John F. Kennedy reflected in this book.

Thanks to each of you who work in hallowed historical places, especially Arlington National Cemetery. You labor with heroic valor to preserve the spiritual legacy of patriotism for future generations and are deserving of great respect.

My appreciation is deep and lasting for John F. Kennedy's biographers and is matched only by my admiration.

My dedicated husband Edward, our cherished children, grandchildren, great-grandchildren, godchildren, spiritual children, colleagues, friends, and readers animate all my work. You are exquisite blessings of Kind Providence for which I can never thank God enough. My prayer is that you are rewarded a thousandfold in this life and the next.

BIBLIOGRAPHY

Bedell Smith, Sally. *Grace and Power.* Aurum Press, 2011.

Blair, Joan and Clay Jr. *The Search for JFK.* Putnam, 1974.

Bradlee, Benjamin C. *Conversations with Kennedy.* W.W. Norton, 1984.

_____ *A Good Life.* Simon & Schuster, 2011

Carey, Patick W. *Avery Cardinal Dulles SJ, A Model Theologian.* Paulist Press, 2010.

Chambers, Oswald. *My Utmost for His Highest.* Barbour Publishing, 1963.

Collier, Peter, and Horowitz, David. *The Kennedys: An American Drama.* Summit Books, 1984.

Connell, Janice T. *The Spiritual Journey of George Washington.* Hatherleigh Press, 2007.

_____ *Meetings With Mary.* Random House, 1995.

_____ *Secrets of Mary.* St. Martin's Press, 2009.

_____ *Christ Through Mary.* Four Winds Publishing, 2021.

_____ *Mary Seat of Wisdom.* Four Winds Publishing, 2022.

Cousins, Norman, *The Improbable Triumvirate.* W.W. Norton & Company, 1972.

Dallek, Robert. *An Unfinished Life.* Back Bay Books, 2003.

Damore, Leo. *The Cape Cod Years of John Fitzgerald Kennedy.* Prentice Hall, 1967.

Davids, Jules. *America and the World of Our Time US Diplomacy in the Twentieth Century.* Random House, 1960.

Davis, John H. *The Kennedys.* McGraw Hill, 1984.

Dobbs, Michael. *One Minute to Midnight.* Arrow Books, 2009.

Donaldson, Gary. *The First Modern Campaign.* Rowman & Littlefield, 2007.

Eagan, Timothy. *Fever in the Heartland.* Viking, 2023.

Ferguson, Thomas P. *Catholic and American: The Political Theology of John Courtney Murray.* Sheed & Ward, 1993.

Fisher, James T. *Communion of Immigrants,* Oxford University Press, 2000.

Freedman, Lawrence. *Kennedy's Wars.* Oxford University Press, 2000.

Goodwin, Doris Kearns. *Fitzgeralds and Kennedys.* Simon & Schuster, 1987.

Hamilton, Nigel. *JFK: Reckless Youth.* Random House, 1992.

Hersh, Seymore. *The Dark Side of Camelot.* Little Brown, 1997.

Hannan, Philip. *The Archbishop Wore Combat Boots.* Our Sunday Visitor, 2010.

Hebblethwaite, Peter. *Pope John XXIII.* Doubleday, 1984.

Heckler, Kimberly. *A Woman of Firsts, Margaret Heckler, Political Trailblazer.* Lyons Press, 2025.

Hennesey, James. *American Catholics.* Oxford University Press, 1981.

BIBLIOGRAPHY

John XXIII, Pope Saint. *Journal of a Soul*. Image Books, 1965.

Kaiser, Robert B. *Pope John XXIII*. Macmillan, 1963.

Kengor, Paul. *The Devil and Karl Marx*. Tan Books, 2020.

Kennedy, Edward M. *True Compass*. Hachette Book Group, 2009.

Kennedy, Jacqueline. *Historic Conversations on Life with John F. Kennedy, Interviews with Arthur M. Schlesinger, Jr. 1964*. Hyperion, 2011.

Kennedy, John F. *Profiles in Courage*. Harper & Brothers, 1957.

Kennedy, Robert F. *Thirteen Days, A Memoir of the Cuban Missile Crisis*. W.W. Norton & Company, Inc., 1969.

Kennedy, Rose Fitzgerald. *Times to Remember*. Doubleday, 1974.

Kostlevy, William. *Historical Dictionary of the Holiness Movement*. Scarecrow Press, 2009.

Khruschev, Nikita. *Khruschev Remembers*. Little Brown & Co., 1970.

Leamer, Lawrence. *The Kennedy Men: 1901-1963*. William Morrow, 2002.

Ling, Peter. *John F. Kennedy*. Routledge, 2013.

Lovasik, Lawrence. *The Hidden Power of Kindness*. Sophia Press, 1962, 1999.

Manchester, William. *The Death of a President*. Harper & Row, 1967.

Meacham, Jon. *Thomas Jefferson: The Art of Power*. Random House, 2012.

Meacham, Jon. *American Lion: Andrew Jackson in the White House*. Random House, 2009.

Matthews, Chris. *Bobby Kennedy*. Simon & Schuster, 2017.

_____. *Jack Kennedy: Illusive Hero*. Simon & Schuster, 2011.

McKean, David. *Tommy the Cork*. Steerforth Press, 2004.

McKeon, Kathy. *Jackie's Girl*. Gallery Books, 2017.

McHugh, John A. & Callan, Charles J. Trans. *Catechism of the Catholic Church*. Tan Books, 1982.

Miscamble, Wilson D. *American Priest*. Image, 2019.

Montague, Charlotte. *Kennedy*. Chartwell Books, 2017.

Montgomery, Ruth. *A Gift of Prophesy: The Phenomenal Jeane Dixon*. William Morrow & Company, 1965.

Murray, John Courtney SJ. *Religious Liberty*. John Knox Press, 1993.

_____ *We Hold These Truths*. Sheed & Ward, 2005.

Nasaw, David. *The Patriarch*. The Penguin Press, 1912.

Peterson, Jordan B. *We Who Wrestle With God*. Penguin Random House, 2024.

Perry, Barbara A. *Rose Kennedy*. W.W. Norton, 2013.

Perry, Paul. *Dali's Fatima Secret*. Sakkara Books, 2020.

Rosenberg, Tina. *The Haunted Land*. Random House, 1995.

Schlesinger, Jr., Arthur M. *A Thousand Days*. Houghton Mifflin, 1965.

_____. *Robert Kennedy and His Times*. Houghton Mifflin, 1978.

_____ *The Letters of Arthur Schlesinger, Jr*. Random House, 2013.

BIBLIOGRAPHY

Shea, John Gilmary. *A History of the Catholic Church in the United States.* 1890.

Sheen, Archbishop Fulton J. *Book of Sacraments.* Manchester, Sophia Press, 2021.

Sorensen, Ted. *Counselor.* Harper Collins, 2008.

_____. *Kennedy.* Harper Perennial, 1965.

_____ (Ed). *Let the Word Go Forth.* Delacorte Press, 1988.

Talbot, David. *Brothers.* Free Press, 2007.

Taraborrelli, J. Randy. *JFK Public, Private, Secret.* St. Martins Press, 2025.

Tobin, Greg. *The Good Pope.* Harper One, 2012.

Third Council of Baltimore. *The Baltimore Catechism.* Pantianos Classics, 1891.

Thomas, Evan. *Robert Kennedy: His Life.* Simon & Schuster, 2000.

Tye, Larry. *Bobby Kennedy.* Random House, 2016.

White, Theodore H. *The Making of the President, 1960.* Atheneum, 1961.

Youssoupoff, Prince Felix. *Lost Splendor.* G. P. Putnam's and Sons, 1953.

NOTES

1. Ecclesiastes 3:1 A favorite Scripture of the Kennedy family.
2. John F. Kennedy, *Profiles in Courage*, (Harper Perennial 1955), 51.
3. Matthew 12:36–37.
4. See Chapter One *supra*.
5. 2 Corinthians 1:4.
6. Aeschylus, c. 525 BC, Greek Tragedian noted: "In our sleep, pain which cannot forget falls drop by drop upon the heart until, in our own despair, against our wills, comes wisdom through the awful grace of God." Agamemnon1, 176.
7. Psalm 145:8.
8. Philippians 4:13; Psalm 28:7.
9. Presidential Historian Arthur Schlesinger, Jr.
10. Philippians 4:13.
11. Rose Fitzgerald Kennedy, *Times to Remember* (Doubleday 1974), 1-2.
12. The Roman Catholic Church retains nobility as part of the Papal Household, and also the right of Pontiffs to confer titles such as prince, duke, count or countess on whomever they choose. The title "Countess of the Holy Roman Church" was conferred upon Rose Kennedy by Pope Pius XII. See the Papal Letter of Pope Sant Paul VI, *Pontificalis Domus* for more information.
13. Timothy Williamson FBA, *Doing Philosophy: From Common Curiosity to Logical Reasoning* (Oxford University Press 2018) at https//www.philosophy.ox.ac.uk/people/timothy-williamson.
14. Arthur Schlesinger, Jr. *A Thousand Days* (Houghton Mifflin Co. 1965), 111.

15 Schlesinger, 111.
16 Doris Kearns Goodwin, *The Fitzgeralds and the Kennedys*, (Simon & Schuster 1987), 735. Author interview with Joseph Sweeny, SJ.
17 Excerpt from President John F. Kennedy's Inaugural Address in January of 1961.
18 It is estimated that one million died from famine or hunger-related disease in Ireland between 1845 and 1851. Another million plus emigrated to the United States at that time. Approximately 35,000 to 50,000 Irish emigrants settled in Boston.
19 Barbara A. Perry, *Rose Kennedy* (W.W. Norton & Company 2013), 23.
20 David Nasaw, *The Patriarch* (The Penguin Press 2012), xx.
21 Nasaw, 23.
22 Nasaw, 21.
23 Nasaw, 27.
24 Nasaw.
25 Nasaw, 33-34.
26 Blaise Pascal, *Pensées*, c. 1690.
27 Goodwin, *Fitzgeralds and the Kennedys*, 237.
28 Goodwin.
29 Nasaw, *The Patriarch*, 52.
30 Nasaw.
31 Nasaw, 66.
32 Nasaw, 71.
33 Nasaw, 80.
34 Perry, *Rose Kennedy*, 50; Rose would have been aware of the scripture regarding Jesus Christ during His Sermon on the Mount as quoted in Matthew 5:48: "Be perfect, therefore, as your heavenly Father is perfect." Parents of the times, especially dedicated Christians, struggled to achieve this goal on behalf of themselves and their children.

NOTES

35 Luke 23:34.

36 Perry, *Rose Kennedy*, 6.

37 Rose Kennedy lived to the age of 104.

38 Jacqueline Kennedy, *Historic Conversations on Life with John F. Kennedy*, (Hyperion 2011), 102, 143, 185, 189, 191, 213; Mrs. Kennedy's observations to Arthur M. Schlesinger, Jr.

39 Perry, *Rose Kennedy*, 12.

40 In 1900, 30 percent of newborns died before their first birthday. Due to advancements in public health, social programs for the poor, and improved sanitation, by the 1920s, and early 1930s, approximately only 9 percent of infants did not survive the first year of their lives.

41 Kennedy, *Times to Remember*, 131.

42 Teachings of both Saint Augustine and Saint John Damascene.

43 John 12:32.

44 Although P. J. Kennedy and Honey Fitz and their wives were stalwart believers who prayed along with Joe and Rose from a distance, their prayers through Christ for JFK were no less effective according to Church Father Saint John Damascene.

45 Kennedy, *Times to Remember*, 133.

46 John 1:22-42, 6; Romans 8:28; 2 Corinthians 1:4.

47 David Talbot, *Brothers: The Hidden Story of the Kennedy Years* (Free Press 2007), 253; Norman Cousins, *The Improbable Triumvirate* (W.W. Norton & Company 1972), 17.

48 Kennedy, *Times to Remember*, 287; Nasaw, *The Patriarch*, 47-48.

49 David Nasaw, *The Patriarch*, 48.

50 Perry, *Rose Kennedy*, 12; Marian devotion was part of Catholic school curriculum at the time. The Religious Sister of the Sacred Heart [of Jesus] promoted this devotion and awarded a special medal of recognition to students who best exemplified the qualities of little brothers and sisters of Jesus. Rose Fitzgerald had earned

such a medal at her convent school in Holland. Children of Mary did their utmost then as now to inculcate Christian virtues, not only in themselves, but also in their families, homes and work environments.

51 *Consecration to Jesus, the Incarnate Wisdom*, as recorded in Saint Louis de Montfort, *True Devotion to Mary* (1941, reprint, Rockford, Ill: Tan Books 1985), 28, 196-199. This devotion to Jesus Christ would later be promulgated worldwide during the pontificate of Pope Saint John Paul II and is contained in Appendix Two *supra*.

52 Joseph Sweeney SJ, Georgetown University Medical Center.

53 Each generation possesses more enlightened medical knowledge. Illnesses of the past however are merely conjecturable.

54 This spiritual charism is a world-wide phenomenon among people of all nations. Being Children of Mary is considered a singular mercy of God who sent His only begotten Son Jesus to redeem fallen humankind at Calvary. Children of Mary strive always to obey Christ whose Mother admonished the needy wine steward at the wedding feast of Cana: "Do whatever He (Jesus) says" (John 2:5).

55 Chris Matthews, *Jack Kennedy Elusive Hero* (Simon and Schuster 2011), 7.

56 Matthews.

57 Ted Sorensen, *Kennedy: The Classic Biography* (Harper and Roe 1965), 591-592.

58 Colossians 1:24. This "life offering in union with Jesus at Golgotha" is a vital element of the Saint Louis de Montfort Marian life consecration to Jesus later taught worldwide by Pope Saint John Paul II. It was an integral charism of the Religious Sisters of the Sacred Heart who had taught Rose Kennedy. The RSCJ sisters and the Jesuits endeavored to inculcate devotion to the Sacred Heart of Jesus as revealed by private revelation to Visitation nun Saint

NOTES

Margaret Mary Alocoque that includes the First Friday devotions which both Rose and Joe and their young family enthusiastically embraced.

59 2 Corinthians 1:4; Romans 8:28,12:21; Genesis 50:20.

60 Recollection of lifelong JFK friend Lem Billings.

61 Richard McSorley SJ was a confidant of JFK's widow and a few of his siblings. He survived the 65-mile Bataan Death March, was a POW of the Japanese in a camp that had little water, sparce food, and no medical care. He was liberated by the US Army and subsequently became a Jesuit priest who dedicated his life to the pursuit of global peace. He told the author that he believed our Heavenly Father allows specific challenges to those who would never choose such suffering for themselves for purposes of soul enlargement that mysteriously brings others to the Kingdom. Richard McSorley trusted that involuntary prayer, sacrifices and fasting are just as spiritually efficacious though often more difficult than voluntary prayer, sacrifices and fasting.

62 Goodwin, *The Fitzgeralds and the Kennedys*, 482.

63 Goodwin.

64 Goodwin, 489.

65 Kirk LeMoyne "Lem" Billings, a Pittsburgh native, was JFK's Choate colleague, an usher at his wedding, and lifelong friend whom Joe Kennedy Senior affectionately referred to as his "second son."

66 I have written about the Shrine of Lourdes in other books.

67 The famous Wadsworth Paul Revere poem is included at Appendix Three of this book.

68 See my book, *The Spiritual Journey of George Washington* for more information on the spiritual element of George Washington's expedition over the Allegheny Mountains. By the mid-1950s *The Ballad of Davy Crockett* was featured in a television series that memorialized the heroic adventures of the American folk hero Davy Crocket.

69   Joe Kennedy Senior had a close professional relationship with the Vatican and was aware of the geopolitical prophesies at Fatima in 1917. I have written about these prophesies in other books.
70   Luke 2:14.
71   See online WWII-Pacific/South and Southwestern Pacific, January 1943–May 1944/New Georgia Campaign: June 30-October 7, 1943/
72   The movie *PT 109* is a 1963 American Technicolor Panavision biographical film of the saga of John F. Kennedy and his crew in the Solomon Islands.
73   William Shakespeare, Macbeth, 5.1.
74   John 11:25-26.
75   Matthew 25:40.
76   1 Corinthians 2:9.
77   Ephesians 6:12.
78   Ephesians 6:13.
79   John 5:24, 10:28.
80   Ecclesiastes 3:2.
81   Romans 8:28.
82   JFK acknowledged that Joe Jr. overcame fear with faith, and he prayed daily for faith stronger than death.
83   Talbot, *Brothers*, 35.
84   Nikita Khruschev, *Khruschev Remembers* (Little, Brown and Company 1970), 492, footnote 2.
85   Last Rites, the Sacrament of Extreme Unction/Anointing of the Sick given to the gravely ill and the dying.
86   2 Thessalonians 3:10–13.
87   Goodwin, *The Fitzgeralds and the Kennedys*, 732.
88   Goodwin, 739.
89   Goodwin, 690-691.

NOTES

90   John 16:13; Proverbs 19:21, 20:24; Psalm 119:05.

91   This phrase is from *The Charge of the Light Brigade* by Alfred Lord Tennyson, an 1854 poem regarding the government-imposed requirement to do one's duty. The poem became recognized as a reflection on the senselessness of war while extolling the bravery and nobility of the soldiers.

92   Continuous Christian teaching of the Roman Catholic church since the time of the Apostles.

93   Churchill biographer Paul Reid described Churchill as an agnostic because in 1898, he had written that he accepted neither Christianity nor any other religion. Biographer Stephen Mansfield argued that Churchill was a believing Christian but extremely private about his faith. Mansfield said that Churchill was baptized in the Anglican Catholic Church of England, believed in Divine Providence, and knew Jesus Christ as the "greatest moral teacher of all times."

94   Talbot, *Brothers*, 35.

95   See Barbara W. Tuchman, *The Guns of August* (Presidio Press 2004).

96   Tuchman, *Guns of August*.

97   John Foster Dulles was Secretary of State under Republican President Dwight D Eisenhower from 1953 until 1959. His brother was CIA Director Allen Dulles; his son Cardinal Avery Dulles SJ was a close friend and confidant of John Courtney Murray SJ. (Avery Dulles was created a Cardinal in 2001 by Pope Saint John Paul II). Murray urged development of a course geared to the "livability of the Word of God" to help people relate their beliefs to the world of their daily lives. His emphasis was Christological.

98   Schlesinger, *A Thousand Days*, 106-109.

99   Schlesinger, 110 quoting B. H. Liddell Hart's *Deterrence or Defense in 1960*.

100 Schlesinger, 112.

101   1891, Third Edition of *The Baltimore Catechism: The Doctrines of the Catholic Church*, 148-154 in effect worldwide in 1953. See also *The Roman Catechism of the Council of Trent*, 363-381.

102   Perry, *Rose Kennedy*, 204.

103   Thomas J. Olmsted, Retired Bishop of the diocese of Phoenix, *Bishop Olmsted on Life, Faith and Leadership*. (TLI Publishing, 2024).

104   Goodwin, *The Fitzgeralds and the Kennedys*, 770.

105   Catholic Canon Law for mixed marriages required that children of the marriage be raised Roman Catholic.

106   *The Baltimore Catechism of the Catholic Church*, #1028, at page 151. The latest iteration of *The Catechism of the Catholic Church*, updated under Pope Saint John Paul II states: "Holy Scripture affirms that man and women were created for one another: 'It is not good that the man should be alone.' The woman, 'flesh of his flesh,' his equal, his dearest in all things, is given to him by God as a 'helpmate;' she thus represents God from whom comes our help. 'Therefore, a man leaves his father and his mother and cleaves to his wife, and they become one flesh.' The Lord Himself shows that this signifies an unbreakable union of their two lives by recalling what the plan of the Creator had been 'in the beginning': 'So they are no longer two, but one flesh.' *The Catechism of the Catholic Church Second Edition* (Vatican: Libreria Editrice Vaticana)1994, #1605.

107   Perry, *Rose Kennedy*, 205. The Venerable Fulton J. Sheen was a confidante of both Rose and Joe Kennedy. As Auxiliary Bishop of New York, the Kennedy children frequently consulted him with their faith questions. He is widely quoted as having said: "When a man loves a woman, he has to become worthy of her. The higher her virtue, the more noble her character, the more devoted she is to truth, justice, goodness, the more a man has to aspire to be worthy of her. The history of civilization could actually be written in term of the level of its women."

108   Whittier, John Greenleaf, "The Worship of Nature".

NOTES

109 Nasaw, *The Patriarch*, 684.
110 Perry, *Rose Kennedy*, 215; Nasaw, *The Patriarch*, 683-684. Dr. Jules Davids of Georgetown University School of Foreign Service was a consultant on that writing project.
111 This deduction is based upon the two-thousand-year history of Children of Mary, beginning at Golgotha which I have written about in other books.
112 Kennedy, *Times to Remember*, 287.
113 Pope Saint John Paul II made clear that human life begins at conception. Consequently, Arabella's immortal soul rests within the Communion of Saints with her miscarried sibling.
114 Frank L. Fadner SJ Russian History Professor, Georgetown University 1949–1978
115 Fadner.
116 Russian Bolsheviks were intellectually unconcerned about the deleterious human consequences of their geopolitical plans. Their goal was recognized worldwide as usurpation of power.
117 Goodwin, *The Fitzgeralds and the Kennedys*, 735.
118 Schlesinger, *A Thousand Days*, 50.
119 Excerpt from The Democratic Party Acceptance Speech of John F. Kennedy
120 Eric Sevareid's observation.
121 Sevareid.
122 Harrison Salisbury.
123 Robert Dallek, *An Unfinished Life*, (Back Bay Books, 2003), 294.
124 Luke 12:48
125 There is little doubt that family money and contacts were legally employed to the fullest extent of the law and significant in the US presidential election of 1960.
126 Dallek, *An Unfinished Life*, 295.
127 See Ecclesiastes, a book of wisdom literature in the Christian Old Testament.

128   Theodore White, *The Making of the President*, 1960 (Harper Perennial: Reissue Edition 2009), 350-365.

129   Dallek, *An Unfinished Life*, 296.

130   Schlesinger, *A Thousand Days*, 15.

131   Schlesinger, 17.

132   Schlesinger, 42.

133   Schlesinger, 109.

134   Nasaw, *The Patriarch*, 752.

135   Nasaw.

136   Cave dwellers are early Washington DC settlers in Georgetown or Alexandria.

137   Kennedy, *Times to Remember*, p. 140.

138   Kennedy. 139.

139   John F. Kennedy, Jr. was delivered by caesarian surgery on November 25, 1960, at Georgetown University Hospital.

140   Psalm 23.

141   Kennedy, *Times to Remember*, 140.

142   Most Christian denominations agree with the teachings of the Apostles' Creed.

143   Sorensen, *Counselor*, 104.

144   Goodwin, *The Fitzgeralds and the Kennedys*, 735.

145   Sorensen, *Counselor*, 104.

146   Philip Hannan, *The Archbishop Wore Combat Boots*, (Our Sunday Visitor 2010), 202.

147   Author interview with retired Archbishop Philip Hannan.

148   Talbot, *Brothers*, 37.

149   JFK speech on October 7, 1963.

150   Paul Kengor, *The Devil and Karl Marx* (Tan Books 2020), ix-x.

151   *New York Times*, June 21, 1961, 20.

152   Ephesians 6:12.

NOTES

153 Schlesinger, *A Thousand Days*, 104.
154 John 8:12.
155 Sorensen, *The Classic Biography*, 249.
156 Sorensen.
157 Kennedy, *Historic Conversations*, 126.
158 Sorensen, *The Classic Biography*, 538.
159 Schlesinger, *A Thousand Days*, 322.
160 Talbot, *Brothers*, quoting Arthur Schlesinger, Jr., 51
161 Kennedy, *Times to Remember*, 322.
162 Kennedy, 333.
163 Talbot, *Brothers*, 253.
164 Perry, *Rose Kennedy*, p 255.
165 Perry.
166 Perry.
167 Perry, 252.
168 It was popularly believed that a "person" in Washington or Moscow controlled a mysterious nuclear button or box that a Soviet or US leader could order to be activated triggering nuclear destruction of the world.
169 Dallek, An Unfinished Life, 377.
170 See insights of the President's brother, US Attorney General Robert F. Kennedy in his book: *Thirteen Days a Memoir of the Cuban Missile crisis*
171 John Haffert, Fatima Co-Founder of Our Lady's Blue Army told the author that he expected a "Third Secret" of Fatima to describe some sort of global annihilation from the "first strike" geopolitical policy of the day. He understood that the bombs had the capacity to destroy the environment of the Earth indefinitely. The eminent French Marian theologian, Rev. Rene Laurentin, told the author that he understood Mr. Haffert's concerns but wondered if the Marian prophesies perhaps involved what he referred to as "personal" Armageddons. Two such instances could be approved Marian

apparitions at Rwanda and Medjugorje, both of which underwent national genocide.

172 Paul Perry, *Dali's Fatima Secret* (Sakkara Productions, LLC 2020), 211.
173 Psalm 23:6.
174 Author interview with Vatican II participant Michael Novak.
175 Peter Hebblethwaite, Pope John XXIII, (Doubleday 1984), 446.
176 Greg Tobin, *The Good Pope* (New York: Harper One 2012), 176-177.
177 Cousins, *The Improbable Triumvirate*, 9-29.
178 This US nuclear Armageddon saga is portrayed in a motion picture entitled *Thirteen Days*.
179 Talbot, *Brothers*, 174.
180 Khruschev, *Khruschev Remembers*, 493.
181 Cousins, *The Improbable Triumvirate*, 12.
182 Author interview with US Army Retired Chief of Chaplains, Major General Patrick J. Ryan.
183 Author interview, Ryan.
184 Dallek, *An Unfinished Life*, 325.
185 Khruschev, *Khruschev Remembers*, 518.
186 Khruschev, 493.
187 John F. Kennedy speech at the United Nations on September 20, 1963.
188 See Timothy Egan's book, *Fever in the Heartland* for more information.
189 Author interview with James Meredith.
190 The televised civil rights speech of John F. Kennedy.
191 This JFK speech excerpt is from Theodore C. Sorensen, *Let the Word Go Forth* (Delacorte Press 1988), 204: to be delivered at Austin, Texas on November 22, 1963.

NOTES

192 Undelivered remarks prepared for November 22, 1963.

193 On the final evening of his life, John Kennedy would remind listeners of his personal dream for "an America that is both powerful and peaceful with a people who are both prosperous and just."

194 An excerpt from remarks prepared for President John F. Kennedy to deliver at the Trade Mart in Dallas, Texas on November 22, 1963.

195 Saint Clement of Alexandria, Saint John Chrysostom, Saint John Damascene, Saint Thomas Aquinas.

196 Luke 22:42.

197 Sorensen, *Counselor*, 356-359.

198 Author interview with Major General Patrick J. Ryan, Chief of Chaplains of the US Army.

199 Author interview, Ryan.

200 Sorensen, *Counselor*, 356-359.

201 Psalms 33:13; John 5:7-8; Hebrews 12:1-3.

202 John 2:1–11.

203 See my book, *The Spiritual Journey of George Washington*, for more information on this matter.

204 Thomas Jefferson.

205 Attributed to Massachusetts patriot Patrick Henry.

206 Matthew 11:29–30.

207 2 Kings 2:13.

208 Prophesy promulgated by Hope Ridings Miller, a close, personal friend of noted Washington DC psychic Jeanne Dixon whose prophesy about the assassination of John F. Kennedy was widely read in the *Parade* magazine issue of March 11, 1956, and quoted frequently thereafter.

209 Talbot, *Brothers*, 242.

210 Ecclesiastes 3:1–2.

211 John 2:1–11.

212 John 14:6.
213 Talbot, *Brothers*, 242.
214 Sorensen, *The Classic Biography*, 748-749.
215 Sorensen.
216 Talbot, *Brothers*, 242.
217 Indian Prophesy from my book, *The Spiritual Journey of George Washington*, 51.
218 This would be JFK's third and final "sign" from the hand of fate of his impending death. The well-known Rosary Novena to Our Lady, which was a favorite of the Kennedy family referred to blood red roses as symbolic of Our Lady's sorrows while yellow roses symbolize the public ministry of Jesus Christ.
219 The first time was as a two-year-old toddler suffering from scarlet fever. The second time was aboard ship returning from England when he became mortally ill. The third time was during a fact-finding trip in Asia with his brother Robert F. Kennedy. The fourth time was during recovery from back surgery. John Kennedy mysteriously recovered from those four encounters with death.
220 Khruschev, *Khruschev Remembers*, 505.
221 Talbot, *Brothers*, 253-254.
222 In the English language, Nikita Khruschev's personal memoirs were entitled *Khruschev Remembers*.
223 Talbot, *Brothers*, 253.
224 Talbot, 252.
225 Hannan, *Combat Boots*, 24.
226 Talbot, *Brothers*, 261.
227 Romans 8:28.
228 Archbishop Philip M. Hannan shared with the author that JFK was aware of Psalm 59:2 and Isaiah 59:2. The Archbishop believed they were guiding scriptures for Kennedy influencing his spiritual determination/discernment and moment by moment dependence on the Lord's help.

NOTES

229 Luke 6:31; Matthew 7:12.

230 2 Timothy 4:7.

231 Matthew 13:46.

232 John F. Kennedy's inaugural address on January 20, 1961, is available for download on Project Gutenberg and is available from the John F. Kennedy Presidential Library and Museum website, along with a transcript in fourteen languages.

233 John 17:25–26.

234 John 14:6.

235 John 19:25–27.

236 John 2:1–12.

237 *Life Consecration to Jesus Christ through Mary* by St. Louis de Montfort, as taught by Pope Saint John Paul II.

238 Henry Wadsworth Longfellow, New England poet (1807–1882).

239 John F. Kennedy Peace Speech at American University on June 10, 1963

240 Excerpt from John F. Kennedy Peace Speech at American University on June 10, 1963

www.ingramcontent.com/pod-product-compliance
Lightning Source LLC
Chambersburg PA
CBHW071958070526
44583CB00015B/1246